GRIEZMANN

GRIEZMANN

Updated Edition

LUCA CAIOLI
&
CYRIL COLLOT

ICON

This edition published in the UK in 2018
by Icon Books Ltd, Omnibus Business Centre,
39–41 North Road, London N7 9DP
email: info@iconbooks.com
www.iconbooks.com

First published in the UK in 2017 by Icon Books Ltd

Sold in the UK, Europe and Asia
by Faber & Faber Ltd, Bloomsbury House,
74–77 Great Russell Street,
London WC1B 3DA or their agents

Distributed in the UK, Europe and Asia
by Grantham Book Services, Trent Road, Grantham NG31 7XQ

Distributed in the USA
by Publishers Group West,
1700 Fourth Street, Berkeley, CA 94710

Distributed in Australia and New Zealand
by Allen & Unwin Pty Ltd,
PO Box 8500, 83 Alexander Street,
Crows Nest, NSW 2065

Distributed in South Africa
by Jonathan Ball, Office B4, The District,
41 Sir Lowry Road, Woodstock 7925

Distributed in India by Penguin Books India,
7th Floor, Infinity Tower – C, DLF Cyber City,
Gurgaon 122002, Haryana

Distributed in Canada by Publishers Group Canada,
76 Stafford Street, Unit 300
Toronto, Ontario M6J 2S1

ISBN: 978-178578-426-2

Typeset in New Baskerville by Marie Doherty

Printed and bound in Great Britain by Clays Ltd, Elcograf S.p.A.

About the authors

Luca Caioli is the bestselling author of *Messi, Ronaldo* and *Neymar*. A renowned Italian sports journalist, he lives in Spain.

Cyril Collot is a French sports journalist. He is the author of several books and documentaries about French football, and the bestselling biographies *Pogba, Martial* and *Mbappé*.

Contents

Chapter 1

A Family Passion

1950, Paços de Ferreira, Portugal. The story begins here, in a village 28 kilometres from Porto with 53,000 inhabitants, known as the *Capital do Móvel* (Capital of Furniture) thanks to its many furniture factories; it even has its own Ikea.

It is on 5 April in the Holy Year proclaimed by Pope Pius XII that the directors of the football section of the local scout troop realise that the moment has come to take things seriously. They decide, after decades of popular football without a real club or league participation, that it is time to roll up their sleeves.

They take it upon themselves to found the Futebol Clube Vasco de Gama. The name is both a tribute to the Portuguese navigator and explorer and a nod to the Club De Regatas Vasco de Gama in Rio de Janeiro, a Brazilian football institution founded in 1898 by Portuguese immigrants. In the 1940s and 50s, they set the Carioca championship ablaze. Two names stood out: Barbosa, the *canariña* keeper who would never be forgiven after the *Maracanazo* – the 1950 World Cup final loss to Uruguay – and Vavà, the striker who was part of the sing-song trio for the Brazilian national team: Didì, Vavà, Pelè. In short, the name chosen by the scouts had a ring to it and would bring them good luck.

Their strip was yellow, with a Maltese cross on the chest, blue shorts and socks. After registering its name, social status, colours and structure in black and white the club was now part of the Associação de Futebol do Porto. Then came the green light to renovate the pitches at Campo de Cavada and enrol in the regional championship. The team's official debut was scheduled for 19 November 1950 at the ground in nearby Tapada. Vasco de Gama, or Vasquinho as it had been affectionately christened by its supporters, beat Lousada 2–1. In other words, they won the derby! (Lousada is a small town just seven kilometres from Paços de Ferreira).

It is well known that local rivalries were particularly strong in amateur football back then. It was Agostinho Alves, a capable striker, who scored the winning goal. He was one of the stars of the team, as were the goalkeeper Leão and the defender Amaro Lopes, who was known as Amaro da Cavada as he was born in the same part of town as the football ground. Within the family he was known as Tio Mário. He was 27. The team photo for the 1951–52 season shows him in the front row, kneeling as he holds the ball. He has black hair, slicked back with pomade, a thin and angular face with an imposing nose. Beneath the thin moustache of a Hollywood actor he is sporting an amused smile, which changes his features and gives him a deep expressive wrinkle on his cheek. He is wearing the yellow shirt with a laced-up neck, as was customary at the time. As a defender he was described as '*raçudo*', a symbol of the '*garra pacense*', in other words a footballer with plenty of character, one who did not make himself scarce when the game required him to give his all or spit blood. A Gennaro Gattuso, a Pepe, a John Terry or an Eric Cantona, for example. 'He was a tough guy, hard but correct. Noble, I would say,' explains José Lopes, his eldest son.

Amaro supported FC Porto, he loved football, had been playing for years, and took the ups and down of Vasquinho's seasons with a smile. It was a club that, from the very beginning, knew how to maintain good relations with the 'greats' of the region, so much so that to the great joy of Amaro and his *pacense* teammates, Porto and Boavista came to play friendlies at the Campo da Cavada. Later, Panteras (the nickname given to players from the Boavista club) even provided them with a new strip. The first great sporting success came in January 1953: Vasco won away at Amarante, a formidable opponent, and, with a 2–1 victory over Penafiel, clinched the third regional division championship – the fourth level of Portuguese football – although they were not promoted at the end of the season. That would take another four years. On 10 July 1957, after a footballing marathon of four matches in a row with a total of more than six hours of play, Vasquinho fought off Sporting Clube da Cruz and achieved promotion to the second regional division.

When, during the 1962–63 season, the club changed its name to become Futebol Clube de Paços de Ferreira, also changing its colours shortly afterwards (from yellow to blue and white stripes in honour of FC Porto), Amaro Lopes da Cavada was no longer part of the team. Like millions of Portuguese, he had packed his bags and left. With his wife Carolina, one year his junior and originally from the parish of São Pedro da Raimunda, and their three sons, he took the difficult decision to emigrate.

'My parents arrived in France at Christmas 1957. I was four, Maria was two and Manu was a newborn, he wasn't even three weeks old,' recalls José Lopes. 'We were supposed to go to Cassis, where we had family who could help us, but my father found a job in construction in Mâcon. So, at Christmas, we ended up in the extreme south of Burgundy, 70 kilometres from Lyon. We were the first Portuguese family to arrive in the town. There's a large community there now, with more than 120 families. Lots of them, very many, came from Paços da Ferreira and landed up there thanks to my parents, who helped members of our family, then our friends to find work and get on their feet. I remember that my mother, who had her hands full with the four of us [my sister Andrée was born a year after we arrived in Mâcon], helped the young people who came on their own, giving them a hand with administrative procedures and, as she didn't know how to write in French, she would ask me, when I was just ten years old, to fill out forms and requests. Many of those fleeing the Salazar dictatorship came knocking on our door and were welcomed by us until they found a place to live. Our house in Fontenailles, not far from Champlevert, was almost like the centre of the Portuguese community.

'Although she had to stay at home, my mother helped a great many people. My father worked an enormous amount. He worked hard at the building site and forged a career in construction, but never forgot about football during those first five years. He played at FC Mâcon and Crêches-sur-Saône, a village 8 kilometres from here.'

As incredible as it may sound, it seems the Portuguese defender never took his sons to the stadium. But they went anyway, and a passion for football was handed down. Maybe it is in the family's DNA. José played for twelve years with ASPTT Mâcon and had a season at La Chapelle-de-Guinchay. Manu, his brother, a false winger on the right, who is said to have been the king of perfect passes and hook turns, played for the Association Mâcon Portugais. 'He could have been a pro if he'd taken it more seriously,' says José. 'One summer, he had a trial in Portugal and they wanted him. But he wasn't interested in it any more.'

But the Lopes brothers shared this passion for football with a certain Alain Griezmann, whom they met at secondary school in the late 1960s. He was in the same class as Manu

Lopes. The two were inseparable and they spent their afternoons on the pitch. They got along wonderfully and despite the years that friendship has not diminished. Alain spent time with the Lopes family and ended up falling in love with Isabelle, the youngest daughter of Amaro and Carolina. He was 29, she was twenty and they started dating. Thanks to football and Sporting's Sunday matches, they saw each other regularly and were married the following year. Antoine was born on 21 March 1991. Isabelle had Maud three years later, and Théo, the youngest in the family, was born in 1996.

Amaro Lopes da Camada, their maternal grandfather died in 1992. He would never meet Théo. Nor would he see his grandson, Antoine, reach the pinnacle of world football. He would not be able to support his beloved Paços da Ferreira in the Primeira Liga, the top division of the Portuguese championship. But his sons, grandchildren and the Portuguese community of Mâcon still think of him and have not forgotten his great passion for football, which he has handed down to his descendants. Every February, for nineteen years, Sporting Club Mâcon has organised a futsal tournament for its youngest players. It is named after Amaro Lopes.

Chapter 2

The Blue Doors

These two large, well-worn blue doors have nothing particularly unusual about them, except that with a little imagination, they could be mistaken for a football goal. They have now become a place of worship as they still bear the traces of the local boy's first kicks. It was here that Antoine Griezmann relentlessly tortured the wooden garage door. He would spend hours kicking and kicking to train his left foot. If you look more closely at the old family home, you can imagine the rhythm of his training regime. You can clearly make out the ball marks. There are dozens of them, all different sizes. Footballs of course, but basketballs and tennis balls too.

There is scarcely time to scrutinise the door before a man in his sixties emerges from the Parc des Gautriats, next to the house. He shouts over to us: 'You've come about the Griezmanns, right? I saw the kid training. I'm a neighbour. He would spend hours kicking against that blue door. Rain or shine, often on his own. His mother had to shout at him to stop, she was so fed up with the noise of the ball against the garage. But we're proud of that door in this part of town. Everyone stops to take pictures of it. We feel a bit like a part of his success. It was here that the legend began.'

Welcome to Mâcon. It was here in this small town in the centre east of France, lulled by the Saône, that Antoine Griezmann grew up. A small provincial town with just over 35,000 inhabitants, wedged between Bresse and Beaujolais, about 60 kilometres from Lyon. An unremarkable town and somewhere not necessarily used to attention.

'It sometimes feels as if time has stopped here,' remarks Céline Peuble, a journalist who has worked in the town for ten years. 'It must be because of the town's geographical position. Mâcon is almost out on its own. It's in the extreme south of Burgundy, about 150 kilometres from Dijon, but also about 50 minutes by car from Lyon. It feels a bit torn. It claims a Burgundian wine-making heritage but in other ways wants to be as attractive as Lyon. And that's a hard comparison to live up to.'

First impressions of the town are indeed contrasting. Straight away, you feel how pleasant life must be as you pass the vineyards that wrap around the city, wander along the banks of the Saône, admire the Saint-Vincent cathedral or cross Place aux Herbes to see the astonishing *maison de bois* (a medieval timber-frame house at the heart of the city). The narrow cobbled streets of the town centre have plenty of surprises in store for those who have the time to get lost. But, paradoxically, there is also a slightly antiquated feel, a sense of boredom that lingers in the air. As if the town has remained frozen too long, to the point of gathering dust.

Perhaps it is the fault of Alphonse de Lamartine. A 19th-century poet and politician – born in Mâcon in 1790; died in Paris in 1869 – De Lamartine was the town's main source of pride for more than 150 years. The author of *Méditations poétiques*, from which the famous poems 'Le Lac' (The Lake) and 'L'Isolement' (Isolation) are taken, can be found on every street corner. The town centre is named after him: there are the Lamartine Quays, the Lamartine Esplanade, the Lamartine High School, the Lamartine Museum, and his imposing statue has stood outside the town hall since 1878. He is the boss here, so much so that the Mâconnais like to refer to their town as the '*cité Lamartine*'.

Alphonse de Lamartine undoubtedly gave the town its penchant for culture and elegance. Mâcon has a national theatre, a symphonic orchestra that plays regularly in the Saint-Vincent Cathedral, and its own society for the arts, sciences and literature, founded in 1805. Mâcon, like all good provincial towns, is also a subscriber to the rewards of being a '*ville fleurie*', a town in bloom, and was awarded its second Fleur d'Or in 2016.

Would it be fair to say that Mâcon thinks of itself as a little bourgeois? Or rather '*faux-bourgeois*' in the words of a supervisor from a local sports club: 'It's an administrative town with plenty of officials. A town where nothing much happens.'

From a sporting perspective, this does seem to be the case. The most recent popular event of any size dates back to 2006, when the Tour de France passed through the town. When it comes to medal tables, there are not many champions to speak of. There was a basketball player, Alain Digbeu – trained at ASVEL in the late 1990s – who went on to do well with FC Barcelona and Real Madrid's basketball teams. But apart from 92 games for the French basketball team, this does not amount to much. There have also been a few footballers with modest careers: Frédéric Jay and Antonio Gomez, who both played for Auxerre, the goalkeeper Jean-Philippe Forêt (Montceau and Olympique Lyonnais) and the striker Roland Vieira, a French international in every junior category but eventually blocked from progressing at Olympique Lyonnais (OL) in the early 2000s by Sidney Govou.

'This isn't a sporting town,' confirms Bernard Pichegru, editor at *Le Journal de Saône et Loire*. 'There is no mass sports policy. No club has ever managed to play its cards right. Rugby is vegetating and football has never been a priority. At one time, there was talk of one big south Burgundy club that would bring together the towns of Mâcon, Gueugnon, Louhans and Montceau, but the idea was quickly abandoned.' Mâcon would never be all that keen on football, but it is a town by the water, facing the peaceful banks of the Saône, where its inhabitants meet in the summer to attend various competitions organised by rowing and speedboat racing clubs.

Antoine Griezmann grew up in the north of the town, just under two kilometres from the historic centre as the crow flies, in a working-class neighbourhood called Les Gautriats. There are several housing estates around the town centre. To the south lies La Chanaye, a tower block area where Antoine's maternal grandmother lived, and to the north, several neighbourhoods classed as priorities for development, such as Les Saugeraies and Marbé.

The neighbourhood in which this future star of French football was born dates from the 1960s. About twenty buildings stand on a hill that overlooks the most residential areas. At first glance, the neighbourhood does not seem particularly unpleasant. You might even say it was somewhat welcoming. It is a long way from the large housing estates that have sprung up across French cities. In Les Gautriats the pastel-coloured buildings are no taller than five storeys. They are bordered by large pine trees and wide-open green spaces where you can imagine impromptu football games blossoming in the spring. The sound of children laughing and shouting is never far away. The schools are located in the middle of the neighbourhood, on Rue de Normandie. 'Le Petit Prince' Nursery School is a long, one-storey building with red barriers and some playground equipment. About 50 metres on the right is the Georges Brassens Primary School and its spiral staircase. This rectangular building is much more imposing and extends over two floors. It is surrounded by a huge tarmac playground, with faint markings for a football pitch and handball court. There is also a basketball hoop. 'Antoine was at primary school here,' remembers Catherine Guérin, a teacher who taught in Les Gautriats in the late

90s. 'There was a real social mix at that time. The school had about 170 pupils in six classes, but I remember Antoine well. My husband taught him at the Mâcon club. He was a very nice kid who was only interested in football.' At school, as he himself admits, he was always at the back of the class, usually chatting: 'I was the kind of kid who would cut bits off my rubber to throw at my friends, and whenever my mother asked if I had any homework, funnily enough I never did!' Unsurprisingly, his best marks came in physical education: he excelled in basketball and swimming in particular.

Antoine did not go unnoticed with his blond hair and a football stuck permanently to his left foot. 'As soon as he started walking he had a ball at his feet. He spent his free time doing keepie uppies,' remembers Christophe Grosjean, a friend of the family and one of his first coaches. For Antoine it was all about playing. 'He was always asking what time it was so he knew when the bell would ring. He was only interested in waiting for break time so he could go outside and play football,' remembers his childhood friend, Jean-Baptiste Michaud.

At school, Antoine was one of the ringleaders who would make up teams at break time and would even sing the national anthem before starting their game: 'He was a simple, likeable kid who never caused any trouble,' remembers his former headmaster, Marc Cornaton. 'He was one of a group of boys and girls who played football at every break time without fail. After school, it was football again. I had a prime view because I lived next to the football pitch where the kids would meet up. Sometimes it was pretty annoying, I admit!'

As soon as the bell rang, Antoine would dash home, always with his ball at his feet or under his arm. Since the early 1980s, his parents had lived next to the Les Gautriats community centre. It was one of the few houses in the neighbourhood, a small detached home at number 36, where Rue d'Auvergne and Rue de Normandie meet. The two-storey house was rented by the council because Antoine's father, Alain Griezmann, had been a municipal employee of the town of Mâcon for a number of years, as well as the caretaker at the community centre. After school, Antoine never wasted time doing his homework. 'I would throw down my backpack wherever it fell and go out to play with my friends or dash to training. I don't have any memories that don't involve a ball. Even when we went to visit my parents' friends I had to take my ball with me. Above all, football was fun, a real passion. When you're ten years old, being a professional is just a dream, nothing more.'

One story in particular did the rounds at Les Gautriats School. One morning, Antoine's mother, who was a cleaner at the Mâcon hospital, asked him before he left: 'Antoine, are you sure you haven't forgotten anything?'

'No, I don't think so, I've got my ball.'

'I know, but what about your school bag. You might find that more useful for school!'

Antoine could think about nothing but football and his pitches were all over the town, at the foot of the tower blocks at La Chanaye, near his grandmother's house: 'People in this part of town remember Antoine as a little blond kid who wore French national team shorts,' recalls André de Sousa, another childhood friend. 'When we were three or four, his parents would take him to visit his grandmother, who lived on the floor below us, and we would take the opportunity to have a kick about. Well, I say 'take the opportunity'; he would force me to play with him!'

Antoine also had his routine at Les Gautriats: the famous blue doors of the family garage, as well as a basketball court below the house, where his father had improvised some wooden goals under the panels. He spent hours here with his friends, brother and sister. He often played on his own as well. But he always had his ball with him.

Chapter 3

The Nedved Lookalike

It has been pandemonium for several days. Antoine has returned to the fold. It's been two years since he last appeared in public in Mâcon. On Sunday 21 June 2015, the small UF Mâconnais club is turned upside down. The child prodigy has not forgotten his first club, where he holds the 'Griezmann Challenge', now in its third year. Played over two days, it brings together 800 children from clubs across the region. Saturday is dedicated to the Under-9 and Under-13 categories, but on the Sunday this year it is the turn of the Under-11s to show what they are made of.

Antoine finally appears in the middle of the afternoon. He is the centre of attention in his tie-dyed yellow, green, blue and pink t-shirt. His hair is slicked back and his thin moustache makes an impression, as always. Like a boxer getting ready to enter the ring, he is surrounded by an impressive security cordon. Antoine is also being closely marked by a team from France Télévisions, charged, despite the chaos, with recording his every thought: 'I'm very fond of my town. Every time I come back here it has an effect on me. It feels good to be with family', the Atlético Madrid player says into the microphone thrust towards him as he tries to make his way among the crowd of fans who have come to welcome him.

All the members of the Griezmann clan are present, by his side as always: his father, Alain is in the front row. His mother, Isabelle, with short, washed-out blonde hair, and his sister Maud, a petite brunette with tattoos on her forearm, are busying themselves behind the scenes to try to manage the 40 volunteers assembled for the event. His younger brother Théo makes himself more discreet. His uncles, cousins and friends have all come to lend a hand and proudly wear their black t-shirts with the word 'Staff' printed on the back.

It is a return of great pomp and circumstance, the return of a star. Antoine poses for photo after photo, signs countless autographs and receives countless hugs. Isabelle, his mother, struggles to hold back her emotions: 'I'm very proud because I often think about what he's been through'. Everyone at the club remembers the chaotic journey he has been on. You only have to open the door of the UF Mâconnais clubhouse to discover an entire wall dedicated to the French national team striker. It is a shrine to him. Of course, there are framed and signed shirts from Real Sociedad and Atlético Madrid, but also a whole series of photos that retrace his earliest days at the club. Pictures that Josette Mongeay, UFM's loyal secretary, likes to talk about: 'That's at a tournament, when he was in the *débutants* [the Under-7s]', pointing a finger at the young Antoine, in the centre of the photo wearing a blue shirt at a prize-giving. She continues, pointing at the display of photos on the left of the wall. Here we see Antoine lying on a football pitch with nine of his teammates. He is jostling to get his little blond head into the middle of the crowd to show his cheeky face.

These snapshots date from the 1997–98 season. At six years old, Antoine had just officially received his first French Football Federation licence, although he had not yet reached the required age to make his club debut in an Entente Charnay-Mâcon 71 shirt.

'We started him at five and a half', confirms his first coach Bruno Chetoux. His father trained a team at the club and Antoine was always hanging around the pitches with his ball. To start with, we would only let him train because he was still too young to take part in Saturday matches. But eventually we had him play a few matches before he turned six.' Antoine would come every Wednesday from 2pm to 3.30pm with a group of about twenty *débutants*. The Mommessin ground at Charnay-lès-Mâcon, which has since been demolished and replaced by housing and shops, was just a few minutes by car from Les Gautriats. Unsurprisingly, Antoine took to it like a duck to water and attended every session without fail. 'What was most striking was his love of the game,' explains David Guérin, the other coach in charge of the category, whose coaching career was still in its infancy. 'Whenever we started an activity, he was there. He was so happy to be on the pitch. Football was already his life.'

Bruno Chetoux was a more experienced instructor but was still impressed by his young recruit: 'We could see straight away that he was a good player,' he explains. 'But the most surprising thing was that at that age gifted children tend to be more selfish with their play. Not him, he was already thinking about the team. Of course, he liked to score goals, but he was also happy to help others score.' This attitude quickly made him popular with his new teammates. Martin Voir, one of his most loyal friends and earliest teammates, remembers: 'It's true that he was already capable of dribbling past the entire opposing team. We relied on him. But at the same time he was always very generous and never pushed himself forward.'

Antoine was soon playing above his age category. He joined the group born a year earlier, in 1990. With this team, which had already forged a reputation on the pitches of

Saône-et-Loire, he quickly found his feet and showed himself to have the mindset of a true champion: 'We didn't lose many matches, hardly ever,' says Bruno Chetoux. 'When it did happen, it was a big deal. I remember an indoor tournament in Mâcon that we lost on penalties. Antoine missed his last attempt. He left in tears, without even waiting for the prize-giving. That showed me his temperament. Even at that age he was already a winner. He was determined.'

Because the team was performing so well, the two coaches decided to play further afield during the second year. 'We travelled to compete in more important regional tournaments,' recalls David Guérin. 'The 1991 generation was fantastic, with great players such as Jean-Baptiste Michaud.' But in this team, the leader was clearly Antoine. 'Our little star, even if I don't like this word very much and it doesn't correspond at all to his character or behaviour. He was reserved and very sensitive,' explains Chetoux. 'But on the pitch he was the only one you noticed. Even the parents of the opposing team fell in love with the little blond kid.' David Guérin confirms: 'He would also get noticed because he was small, which at first glance could have been a handicap, but as soon as he had the ball at his feet, the spectators' faces would light up. He was clearly the leader of his generation. He scored goal upon goal at tournaments in Sancé and Mâcon. When we had Antoine in the team, we knew we would go a long way in the tournament. But to think that he would have the career he has had? That was something else.'

In 1999, when Antoine was getting ready to join the Under-11 *poussin* category, the local footballing landscape was turned on its head. There was a merger between Mâcon's three footballing entities: ASPTT Mâcon, a club known for its training, FC Mâcon, the town's historic club, and Antoine's club, Entente Charnay-Mâcon 71, which had the advantage at the time of moving up to France's fifth division. This initiative would see the birth of a new club, the Union du Football Mâconnais (UFM). Although the plan had not been unanimously received by the clubs, as its motivation was primarily political, it would clearly benefit several generations of players, including that of Antoine Griezmann. 'Having a single club logically allowed us to increase the number of our youth teams,' explains Serge Rivera, President of UFM for six years from 2004 to 2010. 'At that time, we even gained players from neighbouring *départements*. That gave us ultra-competitive groups, particularly for the famous generations born in 1990 and 1991.'

It was during this period that a core of players formed around Antoine. In the team coached by Jérôme Millet, Grizi was living his passion for football to the full with his friends Jean-Baptiste Michaud, Julian De Cata, Stéphane Rivera and Martin Voir. 'There were ten or twelve of us kids always with a ball,' Voir remembers. 'And when we weren't training or playing matches, we were at our parents' matches. We didn't watch at all, we would find a corner of the stadium and make goals out of bibs or shoes.'

Antoine did not stay in the Under-11s for long. Just as he had in the Under-7s, he was quickly moved up a category and joined the Under-13 group trained by Christophe Grosjean for the 2000–01 season. 'He was bored with the *poussins* so during the second half of the season, he began to come with us now and again. He got a taste for it. Then, when we didn't take him, he wasn't happy. I tried to explain to him that he was still young, but he kept sulking. To be frank, he was already better than most of them technically because he already had great ball control. Keepie uppies were too easy for him. Antoine was always the best: 50 with his left foot, 50 with his right and twenty with his head.'

Christophe Grosjean would follow his development for several seasons. In particular, the two years he spent with the *benjamins*, or Under-13s, from 2001 to 2003: 'That first year, he didn't really manage to hold his own because physique counts for a lot, and at that age he wasn't ready in that respect. But by the second year, he had begun to get bigger physically and better technically. We were still playing in teams of nine and I liked to put him on one side in the centre left position.'

Those two seasons with the Under-13s were marked by the famous Coupe Nationale, the grand final of which brought together the best clubs in France at the Cap Breton complex in Landes every June. Each time, Antoine would miss out on qualifying for this important national event in his category.

The first year, during the 2001–02 season, his team lost in the regional Burgundy final in Beaune against a small village club, to everyone's surprise. It was a great opportunity missed for the generation that had experienced plenty of success throughout the season and won a number of prestigious tournaments such as at Cavaillon in the Var. The following year they failed again in the Coupe Nationale, though Antoine consoled himself by scoring a stunning acrobatic bicycle kick.

He was more comfortable than ever at UFM. Football was the centre of his world. At that time, Antoine spent almost every waking moment with his two best friends, Stéphane Rivera and Jean-Baptiste Michaud. The small group ran riot on almost all the pitches in the surrounding area, particularly at Massonne in Charnay-lès-Mâcon. 'We would play there during the holidays and on Wednesday afternoons. We wouldn't think twice about moving the goals to where the grass was better and, once, because the goals were chained down, we had to break the chain with a hammer,' one of them admitted. Antoine, Stéphane and JB, often flanked by other friends from the team such as Julian De Cata and Jérôme Belleville, had no trouble rounding up local kids to make up teams for breakneck matches. They could spend hours on this small pitch overlooking the vines, playing out film-like scenarios: 'We imagined we were playing in the World Cup or the Champions League. Everyone had their team and we had to do it over and over again as many times as we could. When we scored, we would try to celebrate our goals in the most original way possible. It was 2002, so we tried to copy the Senegalese dance. Antoine was fond of sliding like Thierry Henry or Fernando Torres,' recalls Jean-Baptiste Michaud. 'It's true, for us that was very important,' continues Stéphane Rivera. 'And sometimes, we would have goal celebration competitions on the streets of Mâcon. The aim of the game was to slide on your knees and set off the automatic sprinklers on the lawns.'

Of course, their parents were not necessarily always aware of what their children were getting up to. But the families were close and would get together regularly: 'We knew each other well because the dads were also involved with football in Mâcon,' continues the former president, Serge Rivera. 'Back then, lots of them, including Antoine's father, would come to the club to train. There was a great atmosphere. We would all go off together to tournaments and the kids were always holed up at each other's houses. Antoine spent several days at our house, jumping in the pool. He had a great imagination and was a bit of a comedian. He was a really kind and funny kid who called my wife his '*grande maman*'.

It was often chaotic in the most modest home in Les Gautriats: like whenever Antoine pretended to be Pavel Nedvěd (the Czech midfielder who won the Ballon d'Or in 2003) in the long corridor he used as a football pitch, or when he was in his room swapping Panini stickers with his friends or playing on his console. His walls were covered with posters. 'He loved Nedvĕd so much he copied his hairstyle. He adored Zidane too but it was David Beckham who was really his idol. He loved his touch with a football, but especially his elegance both on and off the pitch. He had his Manchester United shirt. That's why he now plays in long sleeves and likes to wear the number 7', confirms Stéphane Rivera. There are still some photos lying around in his room. In one of them, you can see him smiling as he sits in the Stade Vélodrome wearing the yellow and blue shirt of Olympique Marseille: 'To start with, he liked Marseille, like me,' continues Jean-Baptiste Michaud. 'But because he went to the Stade de Gerland with his father, he began supporting Olympique Lyonnais.'

At that time, the nearby club became a real force in French football by winning its first French league title in 2002. Antoine's father, a long-standing supporter of AS Saint-Étienne, had contacts at the club. He knew one of OL's physios, Patrick Perret, who allowed Antoine to meet his childhood hero Sonny Anderson during one of the team's country retreats at the Château de Pizay in Saint-Jean-D'Ardières. The picture had pride of place in Antoine's bedroom for a long time. In the photo, apparently taken in haste, he is wearing an OL tracksuit, arm in arm with the Brazilian striker in a slightly old-fashioned room. 'He was proud of that photo,' confirm his friends. 'Ten years later, when he bumped into Sonny Anderson, who has since become a consultant in football, at a Champions League match, he sent us a text straight afterwards saying, 'Hey guys, I was with Sonny Anderson!"

From time to time, Isabelle Griezmann had to raise her voice to quieten down the group of children overexcited by their PlayStation. But she had already come to terms with it. She had understood her eldest son only had one thing in his head: to live out his passion one day. A few years later, his brother Théo found some drawings in which his older brother had drawn himself giving an interview to journalists from Canal+. His mother also found some school work he had written in Year 7, in which he wrote that he was going to be a professional footballer when he grew up. Rumour has it that back then Antoine even got himself caught playing football in the school toilets long after the bell had rung.

Chapter 4

Too Small

He had his own special way of leading training sessions, of projecting his croaky voice to the four corners of the pitch at the broad Champlevert sports complex in Mâcon. He called his players '*les petits*' and he wouldn't hesitate to make them take their shoes off at the end of the session to play barefoot. 'It's about feeling the leather better,' he would say. Jean Belver died in October 2016 at the age of 95. His name would go down in footballing legend in Mâcon and he left his mark on a great many generations of footballers, including that of Antoine Griezmann.

For his players, Jean Belver was someone to look up to. He was a former professional. Before settling in Mâcon in the early 1960s, he had forged a successful career from 1942 to 1955 with Lyon Olympique Universitaire, Stade de Reims, OGC Nice, Olympique de Marseille, Olympique Lyonnais and FC Grenoble. His record of achievements included two French league titles and a national cup won in the 1950s with Nice. But his main source of pride was his one and only selection to play in a France national team shirt during a match against Belgium at the famous Heysel stadium in 1950.

In addition to his playing career, Belver later spent many years working as a coach at clubs in Saône-et-Loire. He was described as an educator, a peerless instructor and a leader of men. Over the years, as he gained in experience, he became the 'wizard' of Mâconnais football.

By September 2003, when he was getting ready to start with the generations born in 1990 and 1991, he was already an old man of 72. 'He had coached their fathers when he trained the senior team in the 1980s. He had become their mentor, and he had already got some of them to come back to UFM as instructors. He was now in charge of their children,' remembers a former club director.

For the 2003–04 season, Jean Belver was supported by his spiritual son Thierry Comas, who had agreed to be his right-hand man. 'I came because of our friendship and I didn't regret it. We had an outstanding season and finished the Burgundy championship unbeaten and with only two draws to our name. We even managed to beat AJ Auxerre twice and that was no mean feat.'

Their performance was rightly celebrated by the regional press. *Le Journal de Saône-et-Loire* devoted almost half a page to their exploits in an article that paid tribute to the 'title and national promotion for the thirteen year olds of UFM.' The daily newspaper detailed this exceptional season for the young Mâconnais players, who had conceded only fourteen goals in 22 matches and scored an astonishing 67, more than 30 of which were down to the centre forward Tunkai Pinar. The report was illustrated by two photographs. At the bottom of the page, the two coaches, Belver and Comas, were arm in arm, and, in the centre of the article, was a team photo taken during the historic season, just before the match against AJ Auxerre. Antoine was one of the fifteen players immortalised for the occasion. He is crouching in the front row, holding the ball with his fingertips. He is easily recognisable with his washed-out blond hair. 'He was in his first year; he was learning about football and at eleven was still very small. His behaviour was impeccable,' recalls Thierry Comas. 'He never said a word and, at the end of the session, he would always help pack up the equipment. But although he was promising technically, his size was a real handicap. When you're only 1 metre 40 centimetres tall and the others are more than 30 centimetres bigger than you are, you can't play. So, he trained with us at the weekend and played in the reserve team on Saturdays. During the second half of the season we began to bring him in a bit and he played a few games, particularly a good half hour in our famous 4–1 win at Auxerre. I used him as a spare wheel on the left, as a false winger.' Christophe Grosjean, who was in charge of the 1991 generation until the Under-13 category, sometimes ended up with Antoine for weekend matches during the 2003–04 season as a result. His verdict was the same: 'His technique had always been there, and, like a flash, he could get past anyone, but his lack of stature was even more important on a big pitch. He wasn't the smallest but he was clearly on the shorter side of the team average and found it difficult to get to the end of matches. Objectively speaking, back then, I wouldn't have bet anything on Antoine making it.'

In this large group of players born in 1990 and 1991, Antoine was no longer necessarily one of those picked first to play. He was surrounded by plenty of good players. Tunkai Pinar was on the receiving end of plaudits – the following year he would join the French Football Federation's Pôle Espoirs for promising young players – as were his friends Stéphane Rivera and Jean-Baptiste Michaud, who were being watched by several professional clubs. There was also the striker Stevie Antunes, also born in 1991, who had just joined UF Mâcon from ES Coromanche/Saône on the recommendation of Jean Belver and Alain Griezmann.

Despite being vertically challenged, Antoine was one of the most promising players in his age category in the Saône-et-Loire *département*. Paul Guérin, who has been the

FFF's Regional Technical Adviser for Burgundy since 2000, had been following the boy from Mâcon closely for several years. And for good reason: 'I saw him when he was practically still in nappies because I knew his parents well and my sister-in-law is his godmother,' he says. 'I had always seen him hanging around football pitches. He was an engaging kid and everyone liked him. He was also incredibly passionate. I was delighted to see him some years later at one of our Saône-et-Loire training centres. We had introduced training camps during the school holidays to allow local players to work on their technique. We took young footballers aged twelve to thirteen for regular half-day sessions. Unsurprisingly, he was one of the most committed.'

Antoine's holidays were punctuated by football. When he wasn't with his friends jumping over the wall at the Massonne football ground, he was at training sessions run by the technical director Paul Guérin, at Gueugnon and Cluny in Saône-et-Loire, at Poiseaux in Nièvre and at the Lycée Saint-Joseph in Auxerre. It was an opportunity for Antoine to show what he could do with the ball and to get up to mischief.

Antoine was a bit of a joker. He liked to laugh and would sometimes pull pranks that Paul Guérin remembers: 'One day, during a session, the postman came to tell me he had bumped into some of our kids in the village. One kid, just for the fun of it, kept running after the postwoman. That kid was Antoine!'

'I also remember one night', he continues with a smile, 'when I caught Antoine stealing ice creams from the fridge. Nothing serious, obviously. He wasn't a troublemaker but he was always one of the risk-takers.'

His determination also left its mark on Paul Guérin: 'One day, at the end of training, I got them playing a quick match. Antoine had a bet with me about his penalty. He said he would do a hundred laps of the pitch if he missed it. He didn't miss. Straight away he tried to get me to do the laps. Obviously I stopped in the middle.'

The technical director from Burgundy also offers another training camp anecdote: 'He told me he had to leave at the end of the morning for a minor operation and that he might end up having to miss several sessions. I didn't think I would see him for a while but the next day, who turns up? Antoine. He was completely addicted!'

Antoine always wanted more. On several occasions, he attended the football camps at Hauteville-Lompnes in Ain with his friend Jean-Baptiste Michaud. Known as the *Stage Hauteville 3S*, it had been very popular with children in the region since its creation in the mid-1980s by a small group of instructors supported by the then manager of Olympique Lyonnais, Robert Nouzaret. The aim was to provide the region's flagship club with a quality training camp. Throughout the summer on the Haut-Bugey plateau, each session would bring together almost a hundred passionate young players. They were all hoping to get noticed. 'These camps also allowed professional clubs to keep an eye out,' explains one of their loyal supporters, Philippe Nanterme. 'For many years they were supervised by the coaches at the OL Academy. And many of the club's future recruits were scouted there.'

Was that true of Antoine? 'Of course. He lived and breathed football and devoured every activity. He was a very expressive and passionate child. You could see his eyes were shining and that he had a dream. To say that he would definitely break through would have been wrong but he certainly wanted it.'

The Hauteville camps celebrated their 30th anniversary in August 2016. It was an opportunity for the organisers to take a look back through their files. On a wall displaying several hundred photographs, Antoine Griezmann appears in a red shirt, black shorts and white socks, sporting an earring similar to that of his father. In his right hand he is clasping the cup for the best at keepie uppies in his age group.

Another trophy for his bedroom shelf. 'At twelve and thirteen he distinguished himself every year in the 'Foot Challenge,' continues Paul Guérin. A modern version of the *Concours du jeune footballeur* (Contest of the young footballer), which helped spot some of the best players of the 1970s, this competition involved a series of keepie uppies and technical challenges. Antoine was a finalist in 2003, his first year, and won it the following year. In 25 years, only two other players from Burgundy had equalled this: Alexis Taïpa (a defender) and Alexis Guérin (a midfielder) who both attended the prestigious Olympique Lyonnais training academy in the 2010s. But although Philippe Nanterme admits that 'his experience at Hauteville got him noticed by OL', Antoine would never have the opportunity to wear the shirt of his favourite club.

Chapter 5

OL, ASSE, Sochaux, Auxerre, Metz

'When he was thirteen, he was a little scrap of a thing compared to the others, but he got away with it because of his technical touch. That's what makes the difference now, but back then you couldn't see that yet. Antoine had quality but there are thousands of contenders and few who are chosen. He went for plenty of trials at training academies but got knocked back every time because he was so short. The feedback was always the same: technically very good but too small. That was how the FFF assessed things.'

In April 2014, in a TV interview for the Basque television channel ETB, Alain Griezmann remembered the difficult path his son had faced. The 2004–05 season had left its mark; it was an extremely hectic year for the entire Griezmann family. Antoine's father had taken things into his own hands and played a crucial role in the development of the future France international's career.

'Without his father I'm not sure Antoine would have made it,' report those who were with him in Mâcon. 'When I heard he was attending training academy trials with his father', one of his former UF Mâconnais coaches confirms, 'I said OK, but with his lack of height he's really going to have to impress them.'

During that year, Alain Griezmann did everything

possible to make his son's dreams come true. He coached the Under-13s at UFM and made Antoine his captain. He drove him to his various commitments across France. He was also his confidant on those long journeys, providing a shoulder to cry on after the knockbacks. Yet this father with a crazy streak, who sometimes found himself alone in the face of all this rejection, kept believing in his son. Lyon, Saint-Étienne, Auxerre, Sochaux, Metz, Montpellier, the Pôle Espoirs in Vichy …

Olympique Lyonnais

Antoine was in OL's good books. His appearances at the Hauteville camps had made a good impression. But it was about more than that. Olympique Lyonnais and UF Mâconnais had been on good terms in recent years. A partnership had been signed between the two clubs. The presence at UFM of Jean Belver, an OL player during the 1953–54 season, had obviously made things easier. At that time, the two clubs came together regularly for friendlies between their twelve-year-old and thirteen-year-old teams.

Alain Duthéron, OL's scout in Burgundy, already had the little left-footed player in his notebook before those games came about. He had been pointed out to him the previous year by Jean Belver, a friend of the family. The Mâconnais coach had given a glowing account of the young player, obviously mentioning his lack of height but praising his technique and feel for the game. It was enough to persuade Alain Duthéron to make several trips back and forth between Lyon and the municipal sports complex at Champlevert in Mâcon: 'I went to see him several times,' recalls Alain Duthéron, in a bar just opposite the Groupama Stadium in Décines. 'He had extraordinary qualities and skill. He wasn't like a centre forward but was a very technical and talented player. A joy to watch. He had an ability to see one step ahead of everyone. In every game I watched, he made the difference. And once he'd scored, he dialled it back a bit to organise the rest of his team. Also, if he was needed in defence as well, he would be there.'

Of course, nothing escaped the shrewd eye of the Olympique Lyonnais recruiter. He noted every last detail of the Mâconnais boy's game in his notebook. In no particular order he reported: above average technical skill, a very impressive left foot, team spirit and a fantastic insight into the game. In the negative column, he noted: a right foot that was still somewhat lacking and that he was a late developer from a physical perspective, plus his parents were barely over 5 feet 6 inches. 'On the circuit we had a habit of looking at the family to see what the kid might look like later on, as an adult. As far as the Griezmanns were concerned, the father wasn't all that tall and nor was the mother.'

With all those elements in his back pocket, Alain Duthéron returned to Lyon with a great deal of optimism. As was the case for every player he went to see, he submitted a precise and detailed account afterwards, to the head of recruitment, Gérard Bonneau. Coupled with his enthusiasm, his report soon convinced the directors to agree to monitor the player individually for the 2004–05 season. Duthéron continues: 'The idea was to watch him over a period of time: firstly at the start of the season, when matches are generally easier, and then later on against the bigger local clubs; Sens, Auxerre, Dijon and Chalon-sur-Saône. At the same time, we wanted to get him to come to our pitches and the Plaine des Jeux de Gerland several times so he could be seen by the head of pre-training and mix with some of our own players of the same generation.'

Competition was already fierce in Lyon. There was a plethora of attacking talent of the same age. This generation was already being compared to the 1987 group, which saw the emergence of several remarkable strikers, such as Karim Benzema, Hatem Ben Arfa and Loïc Rémy. As for players born in 1991, OL counted among them a certain Alexandre Lacazette (who had joined the previous season from the nearby Elan Club Sportif De Lyon 8), as well as Clément Grenier (recruited in 2002 from FC Annonay in Ardèche), Enzo Reale (an attacking midfielder from AS Minguettes), and two left-footed players, Yannis Tafer (formerly of FC Echirolles, just outside Grenoble), and Xavier Chavalerin (Villeurbanne). 'It was my first year at the club,' Chavalerin remembers. 'Griezmann came to train with us four or five times on Wednesday afternoons. He was small and had great technique, but it was his haircut, mid-length and a bit like a cauliflower, that I remember the most. He played in the same position as me but it wasn't in my nature to worry about it.' Although Antoine did not look out of place with the 1991 generation, nor did he stand out from the crowd: 'He came with another player from Mâcon, Jean-Baptiste Michaud. We realised immediately that OL was his favourite club, his eyes were sparkling,' recalls a former OL instructor. 'But when a player comes into one of our groups from the outside they have to be better than the others for us to take them. He was at the same level, perhaps a little behind.'

Contrary to what Alain Duthéron might have imagined, Antoine Griezmann's arrival in Lyon was far from an open and shut case. There was a lack of consensus from the OL pre-training staff, some of whom preferred players with pace. Would his size be a hindrance? 'That wasn't true,' continues the former instructor. 'At the time we had some players in our squads that weren't much taller, like Enzo Reale and Saïd Mehamha. What worked against him was mainly that he didn't live in Lyon, unlike players such as Lacazette. It was impossible for him to travel 120 kilometres there and back every day. So he had to be provided with accommodation, a cost that the club was rarely prepared to bear at that age, except for real little gems.'

The club had already agreed to make the effort for several other players from the 1991 generation, such as Clément Grenier from Ardèche and Yannis Tafer from Isère. With that constraint in the balance, OL were not necessarily prepared to do everything possible to attract Antoine to Lyon straight away. 'Because he lived three quarters of an hour away by car and was being kept warm by a partner club,' continues Alain Duthéron, 'the club's position was to keep an eye on his progression. Basically, he was kicked into touch.'

Nevertheless, the Griezmann case rapidly resurfaced at OL. During the 2004–05 season, Serge Rivera, the president of UF Mâcon, found himself in the offices at Gerland to witness the signature of his son, Stéphane, who was a year older than Antoine Griezmann: 'I was in the office with Alain Duthéron, Gérard Bonneau and Alain Olio, the then director of the training academy. I told them that day that it would benefit all parties concerned to have Antoine sign a non-solicitation agreement, known as an NSA. That would allow him to stay at Mâcon for another year and would give OL an option on the player while they waited for him to join the club a year later. They weren't all that convinced at the beginning because an NSA is usually intended for players coming from much further away, often from the Paris region. But they eventually accepted.'

And so it was that the Lyonnais delegation of Alain Duthéron and Gérard Bonneau went to Mâcon a few weeks later. The meeting that was intended to seal the deal between the various parties was set for one evening at the UF Mâcon clubhouse. Alain and Isabelle Griezmann were accompanied by the president of UFM, Serge Rivera, who remembers the details of the interview:

'The meeting was friendly and relaxed. The two sides had established good relations and were fond of each other. After some pleasantries, the representatives of Olympique Lyonnais eventually laid out the scenario they had in mind. The idea was simple: Antoine would stay with his family for one more year, finish Year 10 at his school in Mâcon and play one more season for UFM in the federal championship team for fourteen year olds. He would not join OL until 2006 in the Under-16s. This would leave him time to prepare for his departure, to mature and also to grow. Antoine's parents listened carefully to the explanations given by Alain Duthéron and Gérard Bonneau. The two members of the recruitment team took the time to explain their point of view and asked for a little patience. Alain and Isabelle Griezmann listened without reacting, only interrupting occasionally to ask for more details about OL's plan. After the explanation, the Lyonnais pair turned to the Griezmann family and said:

'"What do you think?"

'After a few seconds of silence, Alain Griezmann started talking, looked them straight in the eye and answered without question:

'"You're saying we have to wait? No problem. We'll wait a while too until we sign then. Antoine's still young after all."

'That was obviously not the response Bonneau and Duthéron were hoping for. I was flabbergasted. I couldn't understand why Alain Griezmann had refused OL's offer. Perhaps he had been given some bad advice or thought he could do better.'

Antoine would not sign for OL, his favourite club. Alain Duthéron was annoyed. 'Of course, I was disappointed. As far as I was concerned it was a matter of course that he would come to us. Would he have succeeded at our club? That's a different story.'

Before setting out to return to the Olympique Lyonnais Academy in Meyzieu, OL's recruiter for the Burgundy region did reveal the following: 'Some time afterwards, I had the opportunity to talk to Alain Griezmann about the meeting, as I had found his refusal really hard to understand. Do you know what he told me? "At the time it was a stupid thing to do but the way things have turned out, I don't regret it."'

AS Saint-Étienne

The other leading club in the Auvergne Rhône-Alpes region was also keeping a watchful eye. AS Saint-Étienne may no longer have had the same aura it once had and was struggling to compete with its local enemy when it came to recruiting the best young players in the region, but that did not stop '*Les Verts*' from having a well-established network. Although they were somewhat behind when it came to Griezmann, the directors of the Saint-Étienne club's training academy were also looking into his case.

It was Jean-Jacques Verseau himself – responsible for unearthing Kurt Zouma (a Chelsea defender since 2014) on Lyon's territory at FC Vaulx-en-Velin – who was looking into Antoine.

'I had seen him on several occasions, in particular when UF Mâcon met AS Quetigny in October 2004, as there was another player in the team we were following, Stevie Antunes. Although he was puny, you could see that Antoine had something the others didn't. He had an ability to see the game before everyone else. As I never go directly through the players, I ended up going to see his father and it was agreed he would come to us for a trial.'

Antoine would never see Saint-Étienne. A meeting was set

for March, but just as they were getting in the car to travel to the capital of the Forez, the Griezmann family found out that the trial had been cancelled due to snow.

'As we didn't have trials every week, we didn't get another chance to see him,' explains Gérard Fernandez, who has been on the ASSE training staff for 30 years and is currently in charge of training recruitment and post-training. Saint-Étienne gave up fighting for the little left-footed player. There were too many risks involved. 'Who can guarantee that a thirteen-year-old player will be successful? No one. Anyone who says they can is a liar,' insists Gérard Fernandez. Would Antoine Griezmann, an OL fan, have been keen to sign for his club's sworn enemy? The dilemma was taken out of his hands. He would not join Saint-Étienne either.

FC Sochaux

There were those who were in the yes camp, such as Gérard Francescon, a recruiter with FC Sochaux from 2004 to 2011: 'I handled the Rhône-Alpes sector, and, in autumn 2004, slightly by chance, I ended up in Mâcon. His talent hit me right in the face. He had something very unusual about him. He was technically advanced and had a real predisposition for football. I wrote up my report for my bosses, Bernard Maraval and Jean-Luc Ruty, mentioning that I had spotted an excellent player. I eventually managed to convince them but, despite his potential, his size turned out to be an obstacle. At the time FC Sochaux had one of the top training centres and already had players like him on our books.'

Bernard Maraval, the former director of the training centre, was much more reserved, although he notes that FC Sochaux never officially turned down Griezmann: 'We wanted to take our time but we never rejected him. There were things about him that we liked but there were still question marks over his age and athletic profile. He was a late developer and was quite small compared to his team-mates. I told his dad that, given his body shape, there was no hurry. We passed these remarks on to his parents and the player. In the end they did what they thought best.'

AJ Auxerre

There seemed to be a consensus about Antoine Griezmann joining Auxerre but it was not in his favour. Although the current Under-14 coach and head of the amateur section, Daniel Duroir, was pushing for it, his former colleagues at the training centre, including the director, Daniel Rolland, were clear: he did not fit the profile of the types of players they were looking for. 'At that time we liked athletic players such as Olivier Kapo, Djibril Cissé or Philippe Mexès, who would leave their mark on the history of the club,' explains Vincent Cabin, at the club since 1999 and head of recruit-ment for AJA for seven seasons. His former colleague Gilles Rouillon confirms: 'It can also be a disadvantage because players with good physical potential make up the difference at the very early stages of training but find it much harder to find their feet in the Under-19 category. Conversely, it is at that age that the more talented, technical players like Antoine start to express themselves. You have to be patient and give them the chance to get there.'

AJA nevertheless invited Antoine for a trial at its Abbé-Deschamps facility. 'He came to us for the weekend to take part in a trial for about thirty players,' explains Vincent Cabin. 'We didn't select him for the same reasons as other clubs. We liked him as a footballer but he was clearly lacking physically. If he hadn't already been recruited by any other French clubs it wasn't by chance.'

'No one can see into the future,' concludes Gilles

Rouillon. 'When I worked at Rennes, we were less about the physique but that didn't prevent us from missing out on players like Hatem Ben Arfa or Blaise Matuidi. Antoine's success is a good example. It proves that recruitment too early is not necessarily a good thing. You just have to look at the players that make up the current France team. A great many of them were late in joining the training academies of some of France's biggest clubs.'

FC Metz

It is Pietro De Cata, coach of the fourteen year olds at UF Mâcon in 2004–05, who says: 'At that time, a parade of recruiters was coming through. Every weekend new clubs would appear. Antoine didn't seem particularly bothered. He told me about his trials and the new training techniques they had helped him discover. That season he played mostly with the thirteen year olds coached by his father, but I had to take him with me for matches two or three times. In particular, he played against FC Metz, led by a certain Miralem Pjanić. That club played a really underhanded trick on him. They must be kicking themselves now.'

On trying to find out more from those in charge of making decisions at the time, Sébastien Muet and Olivier Perrin, a telephone call comes from the club's press officer. 'FC Metz will make no comment on Antoine Griezmann and has no regrets on the subject,' a female voice asserts down the line. The two former heads of pre-training will not, therefore, be having their say. It's a shame; they could have responded to the version of events set out here by a recruiter, Kodjo Afiadegnigban. He could not get over the fact that Metz once let the phenomenon that is Antoine Griezmann slip through their fingers, after he discovered the player at Mâcon during a 5–0 victory over FC Sens. Antoine was walking on water that afternoon: he provided four assists and scored an exceptional goal. 'He did a Marseille turn and fired the ball into the top corner,' reports Jean-Baptiste Michaud. He was delighted as his family were all there watching that day.'

On 22 November 2004, Kodjo Afiadegnigban emailed his report to Olivier Perrin: 'Left-footed attacking midfielder. Very good technically and with good gameplay. Very precise passing. Plays in support of two strikers but drops back and is often the first to make a move as he sees the game before everyone else. He generated Mâcon's five goals and also has good leadership qualities. Medium-sized physically but very significant in the match. URGENT, to be seen as soon as possible. Thanks.'

The message was received in Lorraine. Antoine was quickly summoned for a trial at FC Metz. Kodjo Afiadegnigban still remembers everything about the episode:

'It got off to a bad start. His family were left to eat on their own in the city after six hours of travelling when normally the parents are invited to the club for a meal. That was just the beginning.

'Antoine had his trial. He was accepted well by the other players. During the day I heard two different versions: one that he was good and another that he was too small.

'To cut a long story short, the club decided to give him a second trial, this time in a friendly match against a German team. During that game it was as if he was the only player on the pitch. He did everything. The decision was taken to have him sign with the club. To help him adapt during his first season, it was agreed that he would train at FC Metz during the week and at weekends with the fourteen year olds at Mâcon. This deal was accepted by the family.

'But shortly afterwards, and without any explanation, FC Metz went back on its decision. I can tell you it was a really big blow to the family and the kid was psychologically scarred. I still don't know why they changed their minds. Francis de Taddéo, the training academy director, had confidence in Sébastien Muet and Olivier Perrin, but they were both coaches and recruiters.'

When his father told him the news, Antoine burst into tears. Their journey back to Mâcon must have felt endless. 'Metz is the most painful memory,' he later told the media. 'To start with I tried to take it on the chin, I told myself there must be a reason for it and that it didn't matter if I wasn't accepted by such and such a training academy. I thought my next trial would be the successful one. But then, gradually, it became a bit harder every time. It was really frustrating. So much so that I didn't want to keep going to trials as I knew the response would be the same.'

As he drove home, Alain Griezmann was furious. Nevertheless, according to Kodjo Afiadegnigban, he tried to reason with the Metz directors: 'In the end he called the two partners in crime. He even sent them an X-ray of Antoine's wrist to prove that his growth was a year behind that of others of the same age. But it wasn't enough. The story came to an end with a harshly-worded letter sent to the two heads of the FC pre-training programme. In his letter, Alain Griezmann wrote: "You think my son is too small? Well, we'll see about that in a few years' time."'

Chapter 6

The Tournament That Changed Everything

Back home in Les Gautriats, the failure at FC Metz was hard to swallow. Had it been one rejection too many? The Griezmann family were devastated yet again: Alain and Isabelle spent a long time comforting their boy, before Théo and Maud took over to try as best they could to distract their brother, to lift his mood. His friends also played a crucial role during the 2004–05 season. Martin Voir, his childhood friend, was one of his closest supporters: 'He wanted to become a professional footballer, so although he was disappointed he never let himself be beaten. He never said to us: "I'm too small, I'll never make it." He would always talk very positively: "You'll see guys, I'll get there. I'm small and there's nothing I can do about it! I'll get there thanks to my other qualities that have nothing to do with physique and size."'

At thirteen Antoine was already demonstrating the strength of his character which was vital as there was still more heartache to come. He had just been on the receiving end of another rejection, just as painful as those from Lyon, Saint-Étienne, Auxerre, Sochaux and Metz. This time from the Pôle Espoirs in Vichy, in the Allier.

The CREPS in Vichy (Sports Skills, Resources and Performance Centre) dates from 1994. It is one of nine pre-training centres set up by the French Football Federation for youngsters of thirteen and fourteen years of age. It is a privileged laboratory and a veritable hotbed of talent for the training academies of professional clubs. It is also a very popular place with those hoping for success: they can take advantage of two years of top class facilities and quality training while they wait to join a professional academy at the age of fifteen.

Places are, of course, hard to come by. Only fifteen players from the twelve *départements* in the regions of Burgundy, Auvergne and Rhône-Alpes are selected every year. In Mâcon, three young hopefuls from UFM's 1991 generation were put forward: Antoine Griezmann and his childhood friend Jean-Baptiste Michaud, as well as the team's centre forward, Stevie Antunes.

The first round of trials was held in April 2005 in Vichy, about 60 kilometres from Mâcon. They saw some 40 players come together. Paul Guérin, the regional technical adviser for Burgundy, was present to assess the damage: 'He came to the evaluation tired because of all the trials he had had with professional clubs. His physical tests were also weak.'

Despite the muddy pitches, Antoine was at an advantage in shorter games and against teams of eleven, but he was clearly lagging behind in endurance tests and timed runs. He finished last over 40 metres. It was obviously not good enough. The result was inevitable. He had failed the first test. The doors of the Pôle Espoirs in Vichy slammed shut.

*

Stevie Antunes was despondent. Unlike Antoine, he had made it through the first round at the Pôle Espoirs in Vichy but was eventually dismissed in the third and final round.

There was no question of him throwing in the towel though; he planned to increase his number of trials to get closer to his dream. The centre forward was playing his second season at the club. Alongside Antoine and Jean-Baptiste Michaud, he was one of the leaders of UF Mâcon's thirteen-year-old team. The trio were spoilt by their coach, Alain Griezmann, and were being closely watched by professional clubs in the region. Like Antoine, Stevie had attended plenty of trials: at Olympique Lyonnais, AJ Auxerre and even in the west of France, at FC Nantes and Stade Rennais, where he had just spent a week. Every time the response was the same: 'We'll see you again next year. You need to toughen up.'

A new pretender had been on the scene for a few weeks: the Montpellier Hérault Sporting Club. It should be said that Stevie was getting talked about almost every weekend on pitches across the Burgundy region. With the help of Antoine and Jean-Baptiste Michaud, he tortured the goalkeepers in his category, as well as those of the federal championship for fourteen year olds, as, unlike Antoine, he regularly played above his age group with the 1990 generation.

The Antunes family received a phone call from a certain Manu Christophe, a recruiter for Montpellier; a veteran of the profession. After ten years at Toulouse, where he was involved in recruiting Fabien Barthez among others, he went on to work for SC Bastia and RC Lens. Over the phone, Manu Christophe demonstrated a certain amount of interest in Stevie Antunes but did not yet seem aware of Antoine Griezmann. The player explains: 'My father told him we had a particularly good generation at Mâcon. He told him about a great left-footed midfielder.'

In the meantime, Manu Christophe also received a phone call from Alain Griezmann himself. It seems that Griezmann did not tell him about Antoine but strongly recommended

Christophe come to Saône-et-Loire to scout a central defender, Delphin Bataillard, a young hopeful from the 1992 generation who was regularly used with UF Mâcon's thirteen year olds.

After the meeting, Manu Christophe spoke with the team's coach, Alain Griezmann, for a quick debrief he remembers as follows:

> '"How did you find him?" Alain Griezmann asked. I told him he had an interesting profile but that I'd really liked the little left-footed boy in the team. He seemed flattered and said: "That's good, he's my son." I suspected he'd had me come just to see Antoine.'

Manu Christophe's journey had not been wasted. Afterwards, he called the director of the Montpellier training centre, Serge Delmas: 'I told him I'd seen a superb player. The kid came to us for a training camp but we agreed unanimously that we would not take him. Delmas told me to get him to come to the Camp des Loges tournament in Paris with our thirteen year olds anyway but warned: "Don't get carried away, we're not going to take him."'

According to Serge Delmas, Antoine Griezmann never came to the Montpellier facilities for a trial. 'It would have been good to see him under those conditions,' he now recognises. 'It's tough to judge a young player over a two-day tournament. The games are short, they're shy and get stressed. A player can pass you by.'

Nevertheless, Antoine and Stevie Antunes were invited by Montpellier to take part in the 23rd international tournament for thirteen year olds at the Camp des Loges in Saint-Germain-en-Laye from 5 to 8 May 2005. As was often the case, Alain Griezmann was the driver. As Montpellier was en route to where they were going on holiday, he naturally offered to drive the four hours to Hérault. The two Mâconnais would meet up with the group coached by Stéphane Blondeau before heading for Paris.

On arrival in Montpellier, Alain Griezmann did not hang around. He took only the time to hand out a few bottles of white wine from Mâcon as gifts to Montpellier's directors, before entrusting his two players to the team leader. 'The group had just come back from another tournament,' Stevie Antunes remembers. 'They gave us the club strip. Shorts, socks and a windbreaker. And we jumped on the train to Paris.'

*

The following week in the offices of the Montpellier training academy, Serge Delmas invited Stéphane Blondeau to a meeting to take stock of the Camp des Loges tournament in Paris. It was at that tournament that the fate of the two Mâconnais, in particular that of Antoine, was sealed: 'The instructor confirmed the player's quality. He stipulated that he had had a good tournament, but that we had already recruited for his position. In that area, we had Rémy Cabella among others, who was a year older. If we had seen Antoine in March or April, it would have been different, but he had turned up in May when the groups for the following season had been sewn up. He was a bit of a fly in the ointment.'

Yet again, Antoine Griezmann had slipped through the fingers of a French professional club. 'And not because of his size,' Serge Delmas defends himself in turn. 'But we were lucky enough to have an exceptional generation, with Adrien Regattin, Nicolas Benezet, Hugo Rodriguez and others who didn't break through like Florent André.'

This umpteenth failure would go over the head of little Antoine. On his way back to Mâcon, his dream was more alive than ever in his head. That day it even seemed to be within arm's length. The kid did not know yet that the Camp de Loges tournament had probably changed the course of his life.

In his personal notebook, the Montpellier recruiter, Manu Christophe, had carefully noted every stage in his monitoring of the Griezmann case. These notes explain the rest of the story more clearly:

Extract from Manu Christophe's notebook

(First entry) Excellent left foot, other foot not bad. This player can do anything. He sees quickly and is one step ahead of everyone, his passing is +++

His technique, particularly when moving is +++

He is always in space to receive the ball, he knows how to rally the team, his father is the team's coach, we should get him quickly, he will be a great player in the future.

Sign him immediately after the trial.

(Second entry) He comes for a trial at Montpellier for a week in May 2005.

(Third entry) He plays in the Paris tournament with MHSC. Philippe Périlleux and Stéphane Blondeau don't like him. Serge doesn't want to sign him, I think that's a real shame.

(Fourth entry) I've pointed him out to Real Sociedad. Éric Olhats is the scout who comes to see him at the Paris tournament. He signs for them.

Chapter 7
The Piece of Paper

'*Bonjour Monsieur*, is that little blond kid your son?' The question has just been asked by a man aged about forty. His singsong accent makes it immediately obvious that he hails from the south-west of France. With his build and heavy beard, the man looks like a rugby player. He has an air of Sébastien Chabal about him. As well as Éric Cantona. In this instance, he turns on the charm, but he also exudes a real strength of character.

The parents of Stevie Antunes took a few seconds to realise that the question was being directed at them. Sitting side by side in the middle of the small stand at the Stade Georges Lefèvre in Saint-Germain-en-Laye, they were concentrating on the match that had started a few minutes earlier, their eyes fixed on the performance of their son, Stevie.

'Excuse me?' Monsieur Antunes asked.

'That little blond kid, is he your son?' repeated the man, who invited himself over to sit next to them.

'No. The one with the brown hair is mine. The centre forward. But I know the little blond kid too. He comes from the same club as my son and they're both on trial with Montpellier for this tournament.'

'Your son's on trial with Montpellier?' continued the stranger with surprise, before identifying himself as a scout. 'That's incredible! The way he's playing, you would think he'd been part of the team for ages.'

A discussion between the two men began quickly while the Montpellier players were battling on the pitch. It would last until the end of the game and no longer centred around Antoine Griezmann. The recruiter took the time to introduce himself: he worked for the Spanish club Real Sociedad and seemed ready to offer Stevie Antunes the opportunity to try his luck with the Basque club. His name: Éric Olhats.

'Would you be interested in bringing your son to Spain for a trial?' asked Olhats.

'Why not?' replied the flattered father, while taking his new acquaintance's business card. 'I'll talk it over with my wife but it shouldn't be a problem.'

After one last smile, a frank handshake and the promise of getting back in touch soon, Éric Olhats took his leave of the couple.

Was this discussion, reported by the Antunes family, the result of a simple chance meeting or an approach by the Real Sociedad scout to get more information about the young Griezmann? It's hard to say. When asked about his first meeting with Antoine Griezmann at the Camp des Loges tournament, Éric Olhats has always put it down to pure chance.

According to his version, he had just come back from a trip to Argentina. Before returning home to Bayonne, he took advantage of landing in Paris to make a stop in the capital to visit some old friends. In the end, his unconditional love of football led him to make a detour to the international Under-14 tournament in Saint-Germain-en-Laye, where he fell for the little blond boy: 'Just as I was going to the snack bar', he told *Le Journal de Saône et Loire* in 2016, 'I walked past the pitch and saw him do something technically brilliant.' He also claims he immediately realised that Antoine was having a trial because he was wearing a different strip to the rest of the Montpellier team. Orange socks and a

'Jamaica' t-shirt have been mentioned, although this detail has been denied by the club: 'He was wearing the same strip as everyone else.' Stevie Antunes also claims: 'That surprises me because we were dressed in the club strip like all the others.'

Was it really chance that took Éric Olhats to the Camp des Loges tournament? This is unclear if the revelations of the Montpellier recruiter, Manu Christophe, are to be believed.

'I was the one who told him about the player and that was well before the Camp des Loges tournament. We had met several months earlier. Through him I was able to attend a training course at Real Sociedad with two former club legends, Roberto López Ufarte and Jesús María Zamora. We got on well. I told him about Griezmann during one of our discussions. I said he should definitely keep an eye on him. Some time later he ended up signing for Real Sociedad. Since then, Olhats has been very careful not to talk about how he discovered Antoine.'

According to Manu Christophe, Éric Olhats went to Paris with one clear objective: to see Antoine Griezmann at work. However, the recruiter for the Spanish club could very well have had another logical reason for making a deliberate stop in the Paris region: the thirteen year olds from Real Sociedad were also playing in the tournament!

The 23rd Camp des Loges tournament, organised by Pierre Nogues and Jean-Pierre Delecaut, had a fantastic line-up. On the cover of the programme, accompanying a photo of a young PSG player wearing a crown, were the words 'Come and watch the next kings of Europe!' It did not seem all that far-fetched given the list of clubs competing. France's best training academies were in attendance: PSG, Le Havre, Strasbourg, Lens, Lyon, Metz, Sochaux and Saint-Étienne. The foreign teams present included FC Thailand, Spartak

Moscow, Feyenoord, Borussia Mönchengladbach, SC Braga and, for the first time in Paris, Real Sociedad.

The Basque team finished eighth in the tournament. After coming through Group D with FC Metz, ahead of RC Strasbourg and Olympique Lyonnais, the Spanish thirteen year olds would not make it to the quarter-finals. Their paths failed to cross with those of Montpellier or Antoine Griezmann during the two-day tournament. The team trialling the two Mâconnais players ceded qualification from Group C to Le Havre and Feyenoord, finishing in a disappointing eleventh place.

'It wasn't a great tournament,' admits the coach of Montpellier's Under-13s, Stéphane Blondeau. 'Not just in terms of results but also in terms of our play. This didn't help the two players being trialled with us. I had to judge them on several criteria. The first was whether they got on well with the group. That was not a problem: they were friendly and pleasant. Next was to assess their ability to see the game and find a common language with the others. Antoine played in the midfield behind the two strikers but failed to light up the tournament with his talent. He didn't do anything decisive. Finally, the third question, and the most important, was whether they were better than the other players in my team. And at that tournament, Antoine was not better than the others.'

It seems that Olhats did not draw the same conclusions: 'He spent time down on the ground because he was small, but his technical fluidity made me feel as if, combined with a more developed athleticism, he could really offer something,' he explains.

Antoine's future would be played out behind the scenes. Éric Olhats decided to get as much information as possible about the Mâconnais player. He attended all his group matches against Feyenoord, Le Havre and the Portuguese team SC Braga, then, with his notebook in hand, watched the ninth and twelfth place play-offs that would pit Montpellier against Paris Saint-Germain.

In parallel to what he would see and learn from the pitch, he also carried out his own investigation. His approach to the parents of Stevie Antunes was likely linked to this. Olhats even went so far as to approach the Montpellier coach directly: 'I felt him hovering around me,' explains Stéphane Blondeau. 'We ended up discussing him over lunch because we found ourselves eating together.'

'We talked first and foremost about training principles and the club's objectives.' Olhats had no doubt been told about the many rejections the player had received from various professional clubs, as well as the lack of real interest shown by Montpellier and its coach, who was already well served by his 1991 generation.

Éric Olhats did not let that stop him. Without even informing the Montpellier coach, he reportedly went straight to talk to Antoine, choosing the opportune moment: 'I didn't see him hanging around Antoine,' says Stéphane Blondeau. I had sixteen kids to manage so obviously I couldn't always be keeping an eye on Antoine Griezmann.' Éric Olhats took advantage of a break between two games to briefly approach Antoine by the pitch. What did he say to him? Antoine recalls, 'Someone slipped me a piece of paper. It was Éric Olhats, a French-speaking representative of Real Sociedad. On the piece of paper he had written: "Don't open this until you get home!" Of course, I opened it two hours later. It said: "We would like you to have a week-long trial with us."'

It is not hard to imagine the celebratory atmosphere in the Antunes' car on the return journey back to Mâcon.

Wedged into the back seat, Antoine and Stevie had huge smiles on their faces. They were already imagining themselves making the big move to Spain together. The many failures they had experienced stopped them from getting too carried away, however, and Antoine had to convince his family to let him do the trial. It would not be easy. His father had been burnt by the rejections from the French clubs and his mother had always struggled to accept her little boy leaving home early.

Antoine worked hard to sway them. 'I called my parents, who were still on holiday. I had to wait for them to get back to Mâcon to see the piece of paper for themselves before they would believe me. To start with, my mother didn't really agree,' the player told France Football in 2010. 'My father had mixed feelings. I talked with my mother about it a lot and eventually managed to persuade her. I was so desperate to be a professional footballer.' A telephone conversation with Éric Olhats convinced his father in the end, and they agreed to meet with the agent in Mâcon the following week.

Before arriving in the town, Olhats firstly travelled to La Chapelle-de-Guinchay to finalise the agreement he had talked to the Antunes family about while in Paris.

More than ten years later, Stevie Antunes remembers every detail of that May weekend: 'He arrived at the house and gave me a Real Sociedad shirt. We must have spent a couple of hours on the lounge sofa. He showed me photos of the Real Sociedad training academy on his laptop and explained the plan to me. I would have a trial with the fourteen year olds at Real Sociedad during a tournament in Barcelona. We would even visit Camp Nou, a dream for a thirteen-year-old kid! The atmosphere was so good that my parents even invited him to come back for lunch the next day. He said he would need to confirm, but that he had to go to the Griezmanns' first to finalise the details of the agreement with Antoine's parents. That was how we left it. A few hours later, he eventually called to excuse himself from lunch, claiming that he was meeting friends in Lyon.'

The next day, Stevie Antunes went to the Stade Nord for a match against Dijon with the fourteen-year-old federal team. To his great surprise, Éric Olhats was already there. It did not take Stevie long to find out that the recruiter had invited himself to the Griezmanns' for lunch. This did not give him great cause for concern. Named in the starting eleven, Stevie Antunes found the back of the net thanks to an assist from Antoine, who had come on a few minutes earlier. After the match, Olhats confirmed his interest in both players. 'He told my father he was completely convinced,' says Antunes. 'We were supposed to leave for the Basque country the following day. I was going to strengthen the fourteen-year-old team at Real Sociedad and Antoine was picked for the thirteen year olds.'

On Monday, the two players were getting ready to leave for San Sebastián in the north-west of Spain. They had informed the school of their absence, and their friends too, of course. But just as they were zipping up their suitcases, the telephone rang in the Antunes' household: 'Olhats told my father my trial had been cancelled. Without any further explanation. I don't know what happened in the meantime. But I never heard from him again.'

Only Antoine Griezmann got into Éric Olhats car. Next stop Spain.

Chapter 8
Try Converted

It is the middle of the afternoon and taxis and minibuses are dropping off groups of young boys outside the entrance to the Zubieta XXI training facility. With parkas, coloured t-shirts, a variety of haircuts, earrings, headphones and sports bags, they climb the four steps, chatting among themselves. They pay no attention to the huge Real Sociedad crest affixed to the varnished wooden wall: a crown, ball, and blue and white striped flag. They greet the club official sent to welcome them at the entrance and disappear down a corridor. A little later, accompanied by laughter and a general hubbub, they reappear dressed entirely in blue. They go to the gym to warm up. Spinning bikes, running machines, medicine balls; they exercise for a while before beginning their session. It is not until around 4.30pm, in the light of the warm autumn sun, that the boys finally get on to the training pitches at Real's sports complex. Built in an avant-garde and functional architectural style, the facility was opened on 1 April 2004. Seven football pitches – three with real grass, four with artificial turf – a futsal pitch and basketball court, a 2,500-seater stand, a rehabilitation room, press room, video room and meeting room, everything Real's professional team, *Sanse* (Basque for 'reserve team'), and youth teams could ever need. It was here, at the Zubieta complex, that Antoine Griezmann arrived in the late spring of 2005.

'Antoine was in the thirteen-year-old category, known in

Spanish as '*infantil*,' says Iñigo Cortés who was in charge of the 1990 generation. 'But as I already had two French players in my team and I spoke the language, it was decided he would join my fourteen-year-old group, in Cadete B.' In a ground floor office at the Zubieta complex, surrounded by yellow walls and photos pinned to a cork board, Cortés talks about when the boy from Mâcon arrived: 'They told us he was coming for a week and that we had to see whether it was worth getting him to come back to Zubieta at the end of the season to play in a tournament or some friendlies with the thirteen year olds.'

'Off the pitch, what struck me was his spontaneity. I was his coach but he treated me like a teammate. He wasn't shy and behaved the same way as he played. He was cheeky but never in a way that lacked respect. The first day, he made fun of me in the dressing room. He was relaxed, lively and cheerful, on and off the pitch.' Antoine trained three or four times with the fourteen year olds, who were under Cortés and Lutxo Iturrino, the group's other coach.

'Before the final verdict, to make sure he didn't go back to Mâcon at the end of the week, I gave my opinion,' continues Cortés. 'I said he was an interesting kid, even if he was small and very skinny, and that this was really obvious when he went up against someone bigger than him. I said he should be called back so he could be reviewed in June. Lutxo and I were not the only ones who attended the training sessions, Éric Olhats and other people from the club were there too. In the end it was decided that Antoine would come back.'

Josean Rueda is an instructor at CD Kostkas, a club with more than 400 young players. At the Matigoxotegi ground in Egia, a district of San Sebastián, he finds a moment between two sessions to talk about the time when he trained the thirteen year olds at Real Sociedad. He comes into an office full of cups and trophies, switches on his computer and clicks the mouse to bring up a photo: 23 boys are standing on a pitch in the sunshine, flanked by four instructors. One is none other than Josean Rueda himself, looking a few years younger. It is a traditional team photograph. The image is overexposed by the sun. The standing boys form a chain, arm in arm, with those in the front row crouching on the grass. The fourth from the left sports a long, curly platinum blond hairdo and bears an uncanny resemblance to Pavel Nedvěd. 'That's Antoine, with Real's thirteen-year-old team. It was 8 June 2005. We were in Zamudio, a village near Bilbao. We'd gone there to play in a local tournament. It was the first year, I think. They had organised it as part of a local festival or something. We played three games. We won our group and played Athletic Bilbao in the final. We won 1–0 thanks to a goal from Iñigo Rodriguez.'

Josean Rueda has an incredible memory when it comes to results and players. 'A tournament like the one in Zamudio allowed us to see players like Griezmann, who were on trial, at work and to evaluate them,' he explains. 'These players joined a group of kids who had been together for almost a year, who had already played in a league, and it wasn't easy for them to find a place for themselves in a team that had already been built. Antoine spent two weeks with us. He took part in six training sessions and played some friendly matches at the Zubieta. How did he do? Well. Technically speaking, he stood out from the others. From the first glance, you could see he had acquired the basics perfectly. On the other hand, physically, he was less developed than his peers. From experience, we know that plenty of players, even those who are technically very gifted, fail to break through because of their physique. During the tournament, Antoine showed that he was capable of playing on the left wing, as a playmaker, or on his own up front. He also scored.'

Back at Zubieta, Rueda and the directors took stock of the tournament and evaluated the players on trial in minute detail. What was the verdict? Antoine Griezmann was a promising player who deserved to join Real the following season. He may have been a promising player but he was far from being impressive. 'In that generation', Rueda remembers, 'there were several good players and some were more mature than Griezmann. Like Txomin, for example, a left-footed player. He came from Logroño and was really strong. If I'd had to bet on the success of a player, I would never have said Griezmann. I would have been more likely to say Txomin, Iñigo Rodriguez or Rubén Pardo.'

Jon Gaztañaga, who was one of the thirteen year olds at the time and now plays in Real Sociedad's first team, shares the same memory. 'I think he was playing with Montpellier at that tournament and he made an impression on us because he had long, very blond hair that was almost an afro. Then, some time after that, he came to play with us.' Firstly in Zamudio then at the Zubieta.

On 16 August 2005, after the summer holidays, the kid who was too small and slight, the player who had been knocked back by training academies across France, began his adventure with Real Sociedad. He signed for one year, and not three as the club had wanted, an agreement that could be terminated after three months if the boy did not settle into his new life. His entry into the training academy would not be confirmed unless his coaches gave their approval and, eventually, he would have to sign an apprenticeship contract before receiving his first salary payments. For now, there was no money at stake. Antoine only had to grasp the opportunity to pursue his dream of becoming a professional footballer. Real agreed to pay his expenses: food and accommodation, schooling, transportation and a monthly plane ticket so his parents could come and visit. The boy would not live at the club's boarding school but with Éric Olhats, who offered to take him into his home in Bayonne. Either Olhats or another club official would take him to training every day.

Antoine, who had almost lost all hope of joining a training academy at a professional club, could not have been happier. Real Sociedad gave him his chance, despite being only 1 metre 55 centimetres (5 feet 1 inch) tall.

Back in Saône-et-Loire, before packing his bags to leave for Spain, Antoine was asked by the Mâcon council to take part in the French Football Federation general assembly that was to be held in the *cité Lamartinienne* that summer. The future Real Sociedad player was almost in the front row for the speech delivered by Aimé Jacquet, manager of France's 1998 World Cup winning side. Having since become the national technical director, it was as if he was speaking directly to Antoine during his address: 'First and foremost, stay here,' he said. 'Foreign clubs do not share the philosophy we have in France. Here, we respect our children, their schooling, their family and their training clubs. You will have plenty of time to leave later on, when you've finished school, if you really are good enough. We've lost two generations of footballers here in France because of this policy of leaving to play abroad. We've never seen these young people again, or if we have they've been in a disastrous psychological and physical state.' Luckily for him, Antoine Griezmann did not take Aimé Jacquet's advice.

Chapter 9
A Time to Make Sacrifices

During his early years at Real Sociedad, Griezmann's life was summed up by his trips backwards and forwards between France and Spain, from Éric Olhats's house in Bayonne to the training academy. School, lunch, homework, fifty kilometres by car, training from 6.30pm to 8.30pm, four or five times a week, then another fifty kilometres back, arriving home at 10pm with time left only to have dinner and go to bed. The days were endless. Saturdays and Sundays did not bring rest: there were matches to be played. It was always the same. When it was not the tiredness that weighed on his shoulders, it was homesickness. It's not hard to understand why. Imagine for a moment the daily life of a fourteen-year-old boy, exiled 800 kilometres from his home town, where he had always lived, far from his family and friends. A kid who goes to live with a man he hardly knows, with other young people of the same age whom he has barely ever met. He goes to train in a country he doesn't know, where he doesn't speak the language, playing for a club whose strip he has only seen in a few matches or photographs.

His accommodation arrangement, staying with Éric Olhats, was supposed to be temporary, no more than two or three months, until the boy made friends at the Basque club, but it ended up being longer than expected. It was better than being at the boarding school, where Antoine would not have lasted long. As Éric Olhats liked to joke, he would probably have hitch-hiked home! But, even so, no one could stop it from hitting him hard from time to time. During the day everything was more or less fine: there were so many things to do and commitments to occupy the mind. But, when night fell and bedtime came around, Antoine's thoughts would constantly go to Théo, the brother with whom he shared a very strong bond, or to his sister, Maud, his mother, Isabelle, and his father, Alain. The distance, the absence, the homesickness and the separation from his family weighed heavily on him.

'He would call us in tears,' says Martin Voir, one of his childhood friends. 'He would come back during the holidays. We would have one or two weeks together. We would take our scooters to go and play football at the Massonne stadium in Charnay-lès-Mâcon. He would spend lots of time with us and we would often go over to his house. Every time he left again, it was really heart-breaking. The good times we spent together were bittersweet because we knew he would have to go back again afterwards.'

The journey to Lyon-Saint Exupéry airport was long and, on the way, the tears would flow. Alain, his father, urged him not to give up but often said, 'If you want to come home, you can. You don't have to stay in Bayonne.' In the end the response was always the same: 'No!' Antoine's father reassured his wife, who had long been concerned about letting her son leave: 'Don't worry. We haven't sold our son to Real yet.'

Martin Voir says, 'His family and all those around him were always there to reassure him. His parents played an enormous role. They're a very close family.' But despite the unbounded support of his family and friends, the young Frenchman almost gave up, on two or three occasions, to come back to Mâcon once and for all. Éric Olhats spoke to him, tried to reassure him and, on the evenings when the boy was in the depths of despair, he promised him that if it continued he would take him back to his parents' house. That never happened. The following day, as soon as the sun came up, everything seemed brighter again and the young man began to look at things with fresh eyes. Antoine got out of bed with the desire to go training. His passion for the round ball helped. And even if many thought he looked like a fragile boy, he demonstrated a hardened character and great mental strength. He knew what he wanted. And it was precisely this strength that drove him to move forwards. It allowed him to overcome the obstacles and difficult moments a teenager is bound to face when forced to go into exile to fulfil his dream.

Olhats played the role of father, mother, teacher, spiritual adviser, confidant and chauffeur, driving him backwards and forwards between his home and Zubieta. He took care of everything: from homework to providing technical advice when initial difficulties appeared while playing in the youth categories at Real Sociedad. A perfect example came one Saturday night in spring 2006, two days before the traditional Real Sociedad tournament at which Real Madrid, Barcelona and PSG were all expected: Antoine was beset by doubt. He had had difficulty assimilating some principles of the game. Unconcerned, Olhats loaded the kid into his car for a one-on-one night-time session. The pair found themselves going through their paces on a Basque *pelota* court lit by the car headlights; kicking balls against the wall, working on movement. That evening would remain engraved on Antoine's mind.

'Yes, Éric was like a second father to us, our second family,' explains Alex Ruiz, a French goalkeeper originally from Pau who now plays for Unión Balompédica Conquense in the Spanish third division. As a boy, he lived for almost three years with Antoine in the Real Sociedad scout's home. When he was younger, Ruiz had attended the OL training academy. But it was too far away and, after a year, he began looking for another club that would keep him closer to his family. 'My father knew Olhats and that was how I ended up at Real, at Éric's house. He's a good person, someone very endearing, always ready to listen, but very demanding with us, even when it came to school – one thing that certainly wasn't a passion for me or Antoine.'

In Bayonne, Grizi attended the Collège Albert Camus. His results did not exactly set the world alight. He was not passionate about studying and did not really commit to it, so much so that his teachers often had to reprimand him. The conversation went a bit like this: *It's all well and good about the football, but if you don't make a breakthrough, you will have to find a job and you will need to get good qualifications.* We will never know if this message was absorbed by the boy, but he went on to attain his national diploma and was delighted. 'He ended up enrolling in the CNED [National Centre for Distance Education] to follow a business course remotely,' Ruiz continues. 'We would have breakfast together every morning and then go our separate ways. One would go into the lounge and the other into the kitchen or to his room, to concentrate better. We would study until lunchtime and then go to training.'

Antoine's other main concern was not a result of the distance from his family or school. It came – and this was more problematic in view of his ambition – from how he was fitting into the teams at Real. Everything was different, everything was new for him. Starting with simple things, like greeting his teammates or coaches. When he arrived in the dressing room, the boy was in the habit of shaking the hand of his teammates, one by one, just as he had done in France, but this was not part of local custom and his new teammates found it bizarre. To complicate things even further, Antoine did not speak either of the two official languages of the Basque Country: Euskera and Castilian. Of course, this did not make communication with the group any easier. Antoine could only chat with the other young French players at the training centre, or with Julen Etxabeguren, who had a basic understanding of the language. It took him months to be able to begin expressing himself more or less correctly in Spanish. He also had to digest other changes such as schedules and training methods. Everything was very different from what he had known in Mâcon.

Real Sociedad is a historic club in Spain's La Liga that has experienced its fair share of ups and downs; it was nicknamed 'the elevator' because of its constant yo-yoing between the first and second division. The club enjoyed its golden age in the 1980s, winning the league and the Copa del Rey. It is deeply connected to Gipuzkoa (and its capital, San Sebastián), one of the three provinces of the autonomous community of the Basque Country. 'Real is a very special institution, it is a uniting factor, a place for members of a society that is very politically fragmented to come together,' explains Andoni Iraola, director of the Real Sociedad Foundation. 'This easy cohesion is one of the club's greatest values. All this is possible because the inhabitants of our province see their values reflected in Real: hard work, humility but also pride, respect, education and honesty. Added to this is the fact that most of the players come from the Basque Country and the training academy, that they have all been educated through the same values and principles.'

These values were instilled into Antoine, who was clearly trying to find himself during those early years in Spain. He had to follow the same path as the others, without jumping any stages. His first coach was Luki Iriarte. In his office at the Zubieta, Iriarte looks back over the two seasons he spent with the young recruit: 2005–06 with the Kadete Txiki (fourteen year olds) and 2006–07 with the Kadete Liga Vasca (fifteen year olds). He recalls: 'Today Griezmann is strong and has pace. He's a real goalscorer. But back then he was neither strong nor did he have pace. He was small, skinny and fragile, but he made up for his physical weaknesses with his talent. You could see that he was a different kind of player, one that was capable of finding a solution even in the most difficult and toughest situations. In fact, he could invent a dribble that would win you the game. He had the technique and he knew where the ball was going half a second before the others. He knew how to gain an advantage with his first touch. He showed a great intelligence about the game. He preferred to play behind the striker, but for that he needed to be supported by players who were bigger than he was.'

Despite his obvious talent, at the time he was often relegated to the bench. 'I remember that with the Kadete from Antiguoko, a local city club that trained Aduriz, Xabi Alonso, Iraola, Agirretxe and De Pedro, we went to play against Real Sociedad at the Zubieta. They had so many injuries, there were only thirteen players available,' remembers Miguel González, now a journalist with *El Diario Vasco* who was coaching an opposing team of fourteen year olds at the time. 'They left the substitute goalkeeper and one outfield player on the bench. We were losing 1–0, and when there were only 30 minutes left to play, Iriarte brought on Griezmann. He was small, had a fairly pronounced nose, long blond hair, played well inside the lines and was an elegant playmaker with the ball at his feet. He provided the assist for the goal to make it 2–0. After the game, we read the match sheet and saw that he was called Antoine, but there was no surname. It just said Antoine. He reminded my assistant and me of Guti, the blond player from Real Madrid; he was also a left-footed player and very delicate physically.'

'He wasn't imposing but he knew exactly where he wanted to go. He wanted to play in the first division. It was an objective he had obviously set himself,' continues Ruiz. 'We were convinced Antoine would become a professional footballer.' However, the time for sacrifice was not over for Antoine, who still had to wait for another two years to finally make a breakthrough at the San Sebastián club.

Chapter 10

The Click

'After that tournament he was a different Antoine. He started to shine. It was as if he had something extra about him. I remember I wasn't the only one who had that impression; all the other members of the technical staff felt the same way. We would talk among ourselves, analysing players' performances, and we realised that those four days had been exceptional for Griezmann, incredible.'

On a sunny morning, sitting at the bar of the Hotel de Londres y de Inglaterra, Meho Kodro remembers the 25th international junior tournament organised by Real Sociedad. The large windows of the bar look out to the sea. Inside, customers are drinking their coffees and freshly-squeezed orange juice. It is the perfect place to chat. Kodro, aged 50 with a slender, skinny physique, was born in Gubavica, near Mostar, in Bosnia and Herzegovina. He arrived in San Sebastián in September 1991 from FC Velez Mostar, fleeing the Balkan War with his wife and son. Three seasons, 146 matches and 81 goals later he left for Barcelona for 700 million pesetas (€4.2 million). He then went on to play for Tenerife, Deportivo Alavés and Maccabi Tel Aviv. At the end of a career spent spearheading the attack, Kodro decided to turn to coaching.

'I got to know Antoine at the beginning of the 2008–09 season. What was he like? Small, left-footed, shy, introverted and always hanging around with two young French kids, Jonathan Lupinelli and Lucas Puyol. He didn't speak Spanish very well and rarely opened his mouth. But as soon as he began to feel confident with the others, he showed a different side to himself that was fun and mischievous. On the pitch he did things differently from everyone else. He was very good technically but he couldn't show his talent to the full because he was playing with guys who were bigger, stronger and faster than he was.'

'Everyone grows at their own pace. Some start shaving at fourteen and others at eighteen. Antoine belonged to the second group,' confirms Iñigo Cortés, who was Kodro's assistant with the Under-19s at that time. 'I remember that the previous season, on Tuesdays and Wednesdays in October and November, we introduced individual sessions after training. We called these workshops 'weaknesses' because every player was supposed to work on their weak points. Some focused on pace, others on strength, while Antoine had everything to work on. It was so hard for him that at the end of the first session, he came to see us and said 'You killed me!''

The 2008–09 season was an odd one. Griezmann trained with the Under-19 team but, every weekend, he played for the Under-18s, managed by Javier Olaizola. 'It was a very strange situation: Antoine and Iñigo Martínez were the only players from the 1991 generation who were not able to play with their age category. This was simply because players in their positions were coming back down from the reserve team to get time on the pitch with the Under-19s. I have to say that Antoine did wonders. He was a good worker and someone who was constantly striving to improve. In short, he was a promising player. And as he didn't have the chance to show what he was worth at Real and his rightful value hadn't been recognised, I got in touch with Mallorca to see if Antoine could join them. They were very interested, but the president of Real found out. He came to talk to me and, in the end, for the good of the club, I decided not to take it any further. In March, Antoine joined the Under-19s once and for all and, after that tournament, he signed a training contract.'

The international junior tournament is an institution at Real. Since its inception in 1985, the tournament has played host to some of the greatest football teams in Europe (Ajax Amsterdam, Anderlecht, Inter Milan, Torino, Atalanta, Manchester United, Arsenal, Liverpool, Tottenham, Porto, Sporting Portugal), as well as South American teams such as Boca Juniors and Universidad Católica from Chile. Since its first year it has also witnessed a parade of top players such as Iker Casillas, Guti, Pep Guardiola, Carles Puyol, Xavi Hernández, Patrick Kluivert, Michael Owen, David Beckham, Paul Scholes and Steven Gerrard. The 2009 tournament did not include any foreign teams but six historic Spanish clubs were taking part: Barcelona, Sevilla, Athletic Bilbao, Valencia, Atlético Madrid and Osasuna, as well as a regional selection. The teams were divided into two groups of four and the winners of each group would compete for the trophy on Monday 13 April at noon. For the first time, the final would be played on the Anoeta pitch (Real Sociedad's home ground) and even broadcast live on television by *ETB*, lending more importance to the event.

Real Sociedad were drawn in Group B alongside Barça, Athletic Bilbao and Sevilla. They began the competition against Sevilla on Good Friday at the Zubieta in heavy rain. 'I had my doubts. I was undecided between Antoine and Joseba Beitia,' explains Kodro. 'We had to share out the playing time because we had three games to play in as many days. In the end, I chose Antoine and he scored. We won 3–1.

Antoine showed his true self and scored another four goals in the group matches.'

'You have to realise what that meant for us. When you're a kid and you beat your long-time rival, Athletic Bilbao, finish top of your group ahead of Barcelona and are going to play the final in your home stadium, it doesn't get any better than that,' says Iñigo Rodríguez. On Monday 13 April, Real Sociedad played Atlético Madrid for the title. Antoine was in the starting eleven. The locals created two big opportunities in the first half: Iñigo Rodríguez lost his one-on-one against Hueto, the Atlético keeper, and from a corner, Julien Etxabeguren's header grazed the opposition's goal. In the second half, after only four minutes of play, Iñigo Martínez took advantage of a bad back pass from the Madrid defence just outside the penalty area and fired a cannonball shot just under the crossbar. 1–0 to Real. The second did not seem far away: Aldalur, the central defender, the twins Alain and Eneko Eizmendi and the captain Gaztañaga all saw their attempts fall just short. It was no good, they could do nothing to alter the score. But only eight minutes from the end of the game and at the end of a rare Atlético attack, Ndoye went down in the box. There was no hesitation from the referee: penalty! Jonathan Plaza converted: 1–1. It was a hammer blow for Meho Kodro's players. The match would be decided on a penalty shoot-out. Alex Ruiz, the French goalkeeper and Griezmann's roommate, would be the hero of the day: 'I stopped the third shot and we didn't miss any, meaning we won 4–3. To win our own tournament at the Anoeta, in front of our supporters, was really exciting.'

'I remember the party that followed, the bedlam and the atmosphere in the dressing room and showers, the photo taken in the middle of the pitch and the prize-giving ceremony.' It was fantastic!' adds Rodríguez. Jon Gaztañaga, the captain, was voted player of the tournament and Antoine Griezmann, thanks to his five goals, was crowned top scorer. 'Winning the tournament and the top scorer trophy was huge for Antoine. It gave him confidence. The fact that he had to wait to grow in order to be able to fully express his talent had forced him to develop other qualities in order to be able to compete,' says Kodro. 'What were they? He was lively, clear-headed and intuitive; he knew how to read the game before everyone else. He knew how to stand out, play within the lines and he had a left foot that was absolutely exquisite. In short, he was very good and, thanks to his technique, he started taking corners and free kicks. He had the potential to become a good professional even if, to be honest, I could never have imagined he would get where he is today, among the top three players in the world. What could I bring to him as a coach? Three or four useful tips, nothing more. For me, the most important thing was always that Antoine should realise his strengths and use them wisely. I insisted on that a lot, even though he would eventually have understood it himself, given his intelligence for the game.'

What happened after that famous tournament? 'We spoke with Loren, the director of football. We suggested that Antoine shouldn't stay with the Under-19s any more but that he should join the reserve team for summer off-season training. But fate and circumstances decided otherwise.'

Chapter 11

A Magical Summer

Four lines in the sports section. 'Antoine Griezmann', wrote *El Diario Vasco*, 'trained with the first team yesterday. Martín Lasarte selected the Burgundian striker, who plays on the left wing, to train with the professional squad for the first time. Griezmann, eighteen, joined the reserve *txuri urdin* this summer after an impressive season with the youth teams.'

On 30 July 2009, Real Sociedad were two weeks into their pre-season training. Unlike in previous years, the new manager had decided to cancel the international tour to keep his troops at the Zubieta. The incoming Uruguayan manager Martín Lasarte Arrospíde – a former Deportivo de La Coruña midfielder who had replaced Juan Manuel Lillo – was short on time and knew he had plenty of work still to do. He had realised this on 22 June, the day he arrived at the club. 'The situation was complicated and difficult,' he recalls, now in Montevideo, the city of his birth to which he has since returned to manage Club Nacional de Fútbol.

'Real had been vegetating in the second division for two years, after spending 39 consecutive seasons in La Liga, the elite division of Spanish football. The club had missed out on promotion by a whisker. The atmosphere in the city was not good, pessimism was the order of the day. In addition to the disconnect between the team and supporters, the club was also in a delicate financial situation.

'The only thing to do was to roll up our sleeves and

focus on three objectives: getting back up to La Liga, turning our Anoeta stadium back into an impregnable fortress and placing our trust in young players from the training academy because there wasn't enough money in the coffers to splurge.'

This was a good thing because Lasarte had always been in the habit, whenever he arrived at a new club, of attending youth team training sessions and matches to see the young players at work and speak to their coaches. In 2005, when he was in Montevideo, he had launched the career of an eighteen year old named Luis Suárez with Nacional. But on this occasion, time was running out for Real Sociedad and the first team had already been built. 'We had a squad of 21–22 players and the only position that still needed to be filled was that of understudy on the left wing. We needed a versatile player who would also be able to play up front and in midfield. So, on 28 July, a few days before a friendly against Anaitasuna, I asked those in charge of the training academy to send me a young player who fitted that profile. I wanted to have enough for two teams so I could play eleven in the first half and another eleven players in the second. Bingen Erdozia – a left-footed midfielder who had already trained with us but was unfortunately injured – had been playing in that position.'

The player in question had sustained a back injury the day before in training following a clash with Antoine Griezmann.

'That was why I asked for another player', continues Lasarte, 'and they sent me a young French player. He hadn't played with the reserves yet, so much so that the directors almost apologised for suggesting him, explaining that they didn't have any other left-footers capable of playing in that position and that the only option was this little kid who, to be frank, I hadn't heard of.'

1 August 2009, 6.30pm, Txerloia ground in Azkoitia. The first pre-season game was played against CD Anaitasuna, a team from the Preferente Guipozcoana (the sixth division of Spanish football) that had just celebrated their 75th anniversary. Eight hundred spectators took their seats in the stand. After the first 45 minutes, Real were leading 3–0. And, as expected, at the beginning of the second half, Lasarte kicked off with an eleven composed primarily of young players from the training academy. Among them, for his first match with the first team, was Antoine Griezmann. Wearing a red shirt and in torrential rain, he tried to score every time he got the ball, managed to nutmeg an opponent by the corner post and scored two goals with two good left-footed strikes. The first came in the 69th minute when he made the most of a parried save from the goalkeeper following a strike by Vigueira; the second came in the 81st minute with a cannonball fired from outside the area.

After the final whistle, he was entitled to the traditional post-match interview with a local television station: 'Antoine, this was your first game with the pros and you scored twice. It couldn't have gone much better, could it?' The interviewee, with his sweet boyish face, short hair and wide smile, answered in still somewhat hesitant Spanish: 'No, I don't think so. I'm very happy, I have to keep going the same way. But I also have to play well with the reserves.' The journalist interrupted him: 'Last year, you were playing in the youth teams. This year, you've just joined the reserves but it looks like you could play for the first team. What do you think will happen now?' Antoine smiled again, with a hint of embarrassment: 'There are lots of us in the first team. I'm only eighteen. There's a long way to go, but I hope to get there.' Another question: 'What position would you like to play in?' 'I'm happy up front, even if I prefer

being the playmaker.' Questions were fired at him, about
his background in particular: 'How long have you been at
Real Sociedad?' 'Where are you from? 'How did you end up
here?' Apparently, Lasarte wasn't the only one finding out
about Griezmann. Even the journalists, who followed the
day-to-day goings on at Real Sociedad, were not yet aware of
the young Frenchman.

This 'anonymity' would only last four more days because
the manager, who had originally only selected him for
a training session and a friendly, decided, based on his
results, to keep him throughout pre-season. He wanted to
use the opportunity to observe and evaluate him further.
On 5 August, he brought him on for the second half against
FC Barakaldo (from the third division). Real won 3–1 and
Griezmann scored twice again. This time, the young man
made headlines in the local press. They wanted to know
everything about the young French player whose surname
sounded Austrian or German; this striker, who in two
matches, or rather in just 90 minutes, had scored four times.
The local media were in a frenzy as they tried to reconstruct
the history of the new hidden gem of the *txuri urdin* team,
the real sensation of the summer of 2009. They spoke to
Éric Olhats, the scout who had discovered Griezmann, and
sounded out the technical team who had trained him in the
youth ranks, listing the Burgundian's strengths and weaknesses one by one.

Griezmann was the topic of conversation in bistros and
on radio debates, during which supporters and experts dis-
sected his astonishing debuts. Faced with so much enthusiasm, Real Sociedad called time. Imanol Idiakez, the reserve
team manager, dampened things down: 'The emergence of
Griezmann is good news. It's fantastic for all the club's supporters, but we cannot get carried away after just two games.

We need to keep our feet on the ground.' Martín Lasarte adds: 'I told him on day one, I didn't want the reserve team players to burn out. Antoine had some great qualities and lots of potential, but I wanted to be very careful with him.'

On 9 August, the 39th Trofeo Teide (a pre-season exhibition tournament) was held in the Los Cuartos de La Orotava de Tenerife stadium. It was the first friendly match against a first division opponent, useful to assess the level of the team's play after four weeks of training and also to see the young French player, who had been so impressive, at work against better-quality opposition. To help Antoine fit in more easily – he was the youngest player in the squad picked to face Tenerife – Lasarte put him in the same hotel room as Diego Rivas. 'He was a kid from the training academy. We did whatever we could to look after him in the best way possible and to put him at his ease. He could get by in Spanish but, to start with, he was very shy and reserved and never opened his mouth,' remembers the 37-year-old Rivas, formerly of Atlético Madrid, Real Sociedad, Hércules Alicante, Eibar and now a midfielder with Club Deportivo Manchego (in the third regional division) from Ciudad Real, the town of his birth. 'I haven't forgotten what happened in Tenerife. We had something to eat and then went back to our rooms to rest before the tournament. I lay down on the bed for a quick nap and told Antoine he could do whatever he wanted and that it wouldn't bother me. He told me he was going to go out onto the balcony to listen to some music. When I woke up I couldn't see him in the room. I thought he'd gone out for a walk. Then I pulled back the balcony curtains and saw he was outside, at 5 o'clock in the afternoon, under a blazing sun. 'What are you doing?' I asked him. 'I saw you were sleeping and I didn't want to disturb you.' He was sunburnt

all over, as red as a lobster. He had to put on tons of sooth-
ing cream or he wouldn't have slept a wink that night!'

Real won the tournament against Tenerife (1–0 thanks
to a goal from Jonathan Estrada). Griezmann stayed on the
bench. He would not return to the pitch until 12 August, in
Ipurua, against Eibar. Once again, he caused a sensation. He
scored a stunning goal that gave the *txuri urdin* their fourth
consecutive victory. He picked up the ball in midfield, accelerated and, just outside the area, unleashed a left-footed
shot into the top corner. The final score was 2–1 and it was
his fifth goal of the season. Antoine was the revelation of
the summer, so much so that Real Sociedad's supporters
were starting to get somewhat concerned. They were afraid
another team would come and poach their young wunderkind. 'Don't worry!' the directors responded from their
Zubieta offices, 'he is under contract until 2014.'

The most anticipated game of the off-season was to take
place on 15 August. Real Sociedad were celebrating their
100th anniversary with a gala match at the Anoeta. Their
opposition were to be Manuel Pellegrini's Real Madrid, with
its superstars (Casillas, Guti, Sneijder, Raúl and Robben)
and its young pretenders (Cristiano Ronaldo, Kakà and
Benzema). Benzema gave Los Merengues the lead a few
minutes after the start of the second half, pouncing on a
ball parried by Claudio Bravo after a powerful free kick from
Cristiano Ronaldo. In injury time, Sneijder made it 2–0 with
a magnificent free kick and reminded everyone watching
that he was still a great player. In the 61st minute, the kid
from Mâcon came onto the Anoeta pitch. Diego Rivas had
advised him to enjoy every moment, to make the most of the
slightest touch, to run, dribble and shoot because 'we'll take
care of the battling and grafting.' Overcome with emotion
at finding himself face-to-face with so many stars, Antoine

followed the veteran's advice and played his part in a number of moves. He failed to do anything decisive, but the 26,000 spectators inside the Anoeta were captivated.

Antoine kept a low profile during the last two pre-season matches. He did not play against Real Unión on 18 August, and remained under the radar during half an hour of play against Numancia in Toulouse four days later.

Regardless, his performances in the previous games with five goals scored had already won over his manager and teammates. 'Of course, the goals were important. But what surprised me about Antoine', Lasarte explains, 'was his relaxation, the ease with which he adapted to a new situation. His ability to make decisions on the pitch like an experienced player. He didn't look like a boy who was straight out of the academy, he worked along the wings, combining with midfielders, accelerating, dribbling, crossing well, standing out and finishing with accuracy and power. He had a great left foot and also fared well with his right. All this contributed to him staying with us. To tell the truth, the club was still looking for a left winger. Loren, the director of football at the time, was considering Jeffrén Suárez, a young left-footed Venezuelan player who was starting to gain a foothold in Pep Guardiola's team. But as Barcelona were dragging their feet over his transfer, we decided to fill the position with Antoine. Many at the Zamudio training academy were far from convinced: 'He's just a kid. He's fine for a pre-season friendly, but in the league, it's too soon,' they were telling me. All these objections to taking Antoine were legitimate. But as far as I was concerned, he was so brave, so enthusiastic and so good that I didn't hesitate for a second to give him a try.'

Chapter 12
A Star is Born

As Antoine climbs onto the team bus a smile crosses his lips. He has been picked for the first second division game of the season. The bus is taking him to San Sebastián airport. From there he will fly to Las Palmas, where, on 29 August 2009, Real Sociedad will face UD Las Palmas. Antoine Griezmann is lucky: he has found himself in the first team without playing as much as a minute with the reserves. Destiny smiled on him and he seized this unexpected opportunity. During the pre-season campaign, he surprised everyone with his goals, gaining the right to join the professional squad. It is a fairytale given the chaotic journey he has been on to get here.

Antoine would play no part in the game at the Estadio de Gran Canaria, however. Martín Lasarte decided against giving him the chance to christen his new shirt, bearing the number 27. That would come four days later, at the Anoeta, against Rayo Vallecano in the Copa del Rey. It was the third and final change made by the Uruguayan manager, the last chance to reverse the course of a match that had got off to a bad start. Sergio Pachón scored to put the visitors 1–0 up in the 29th minute of the game, following a stunning piece of inspiration from Michel. In the second half, Real woke up and began troubling Rayo Vallecano's goal but the score remained unchanged. In the 80th minute, Griezmann came on for Carlos Bueno, the Uruguayan striker, who had recently arrived in San Sebastián. A good chance to equalise presented itself immediately. He intercepted a backward pass in midfield with his head, controlled it with his chest and accelerated, followed, hopelessly, by two opposition defenders. He entered the box and aimed, with his right foot, for the opposite top corner. But instead of finding the back of the net, the ball smashed into the body of the Rayo keeper. Barely two minutes later, Rubén Castro scored the goal to make it 2–0 and sealed the fate of the game. Real Sociedad were knocked out of the Copa del Rey in their first match. All the hopeful promise of the off-season seemed to have evaporated already, with the exception of Antoine. Martín Lasarte's speech in the post-match press conference confirmed it: 'I think the boy must have fallen down from heaven. He has something – something special.'

'That's what Bueno, Bravo and I always said,' explains Diego Rivas. 'Antoine was born under a lucky star, it's obvious. Sometimes you would hardly see him during a match, but when he showed himself, it would always end in a goal or a dangerous move. He didn't always have a good day. But whenever the ball came to him in the penalty area, it would always end up in the back of the net. He knew where the goal was with an ease that was disconcerting. It was really amazing.'

On 6 September 2009, the eve of its centenary, Real Sociedad played host to Murcia at the Anoeta for the second match of the league season. Griezmann made his league debut at eighteen years, five months and sixteen days. He came on for Jonathan Estrada in the 73rd minute. In a very dull match that ended in a 0–0 draw the youngster had not been at his best but was still on the receiving end of lengthy applause from the Basque supporters. The level of enthusiasm surrounding the French player was already high and Lasarte was struggling to protect his young striker: six days

later, against Gimnástic, he only appeared for a few minutes at the end of the game. In the following match against
Girona FC on 20 September, Antoine made a big entrance
as a substitute at the start of the second half. He provided
Agirretxe with an assist and only missed getting his head on
the end of a cross from Xavi Prieto by a matter of millimetres.

The public showered him with praise again, as did the
journalists. They emphasised his astonishing form and
declared that there was no doubt he was better than Estrada
on the left wing. The only snag was that the Colombian had
arrived on loan from Millonarios at the explicit request of
Lasarte, who had coached him at the Bogotá club in 2007,
when he was the manager there. He appreciated his qualities
and had seen him work well during the summer pre-season.
But since the resumption of the league, Estrada had failed
to find the right rhythm. His stock was falling with every
match and his place in the starting eleven clearly seemed
under threat. Lasarte had warned him on several occasions,
both face-to-face and through the media. But it was not
enough. On 27 September 2009, for the fifth match of the
season against Huesca at the Anoeta, Antoine Griezmann
took Estrada's place in the starting eleven for the first time.
He kept a low profile during the first half hour, apart from a
few quality touches. Then came the 38th minute. He finally
found himself on the end of a good ball during an attack.
Antoine did not hesitate even for a second: receiving a pass
from Aranburu, he shifted into gear and let rip with his right
foot from the edge of the area, sending a mid-height shot
into the back of Miguel's net.

Grizi ran towards the terraces with open arms, as if he
wanted to hug everyone in the stand. He grasped his shirt
with his hand and kissed the blue and white shield. It was
a powerful gesture to celebrate his first goal and thank the

club that had given him his chance four years earlier. In addition to his goal, Griezmann delivered a fantastic performance. Lasarte gave the Frenchman free rein and he completely let loose. In the 50th minute, he took on Rico, got the better of him and won a corner. The supporters in the Peña Mujika were chanting 'Antoine! Antoine!' Ten minutes later, he stole the ball by the centre circle, accelerated and did his best to provide one of his teammates with a gift of a cross. The pass was intercepted but the idea and execution deserved better. By the 90th minute, when Carlos Bueno made it past the goalkeeper and scored to make it 2–0, Antoine was on the bench. Exhausted, he had made way on 73 minutes to a thunderous round of applause. The manager congratulated him during the press conference: 'Antoine is a pure product of the club and that's very important. Today, he not only scored a goal but also worked hard and showed pace and precision finishing.'

And what did the boy himself think? He was in seventh heaven! A beaming smile never left his face. He explained to the journalists' microphones: 'I've dreamed about a start like that, about a goal like that, so many times. And today I did it. I'm very happy. My strike was a good one. If I tried again, nine times out of ten I don't know where the ball would end up.' Antoine believed that the goal had freed things up for his team and that they started playing well from then on. He confirmed that he himself had asked to be taken off due to exhaustion. Finally, he announced that the shirt from his first professional goal would go to Quentin Favris, his roommate in Bayonne, just as he had promised.

No one came from Mâcon to watch him. His friends watched the match online and cried. His mother, also very moved, had sent him a message after the final whistle. Antoine smiled again and left, promising to work on his less reliable right foot so that he could once again find the back of the net with his '*tonta*' (weak foot), as they say in Spain. The following day, *Marca*, the Madrid sport daily, wrote: 'Griezmann calmed the nerves of the Blue-and-Whites' supporters' while *AS* was sure that 'the Anoeta has witnessed the birth of a new star, named Antoine Griezmann'

The *Daily Mirror* claimed on 30 September: 'Manchester United and Liverpool are battling to sign Real Sociedad wunderkind. French left winger Griezmann, 18, has been watched by both Premier League clubs, while Real Sociedad are trying to sign him on a long-term professional deal.'

Although he was flattered by the reported interest from these two historic English clubs, Antoine was still far from envisaging packing his bags again. His life followed its course between Bayonne and San Sebastián, punctuated by training sessions and matches with the first team. The following weekend, at Numancia, he was in the starting eleven for Real's 3–1 win and played for the entire match. On 11 October, he scored his second league goal in torrential rain during the seventh match of the season against Salamanca at the Anoeta. This time, Antoine took advantage of a creative free kick and a cross from the right to deflect the ball into the opposition's goal with the touch of a real 'fox in the box'. It was Real Sociedad's third consecutive win, taking them to the top of the league. Seven days later, on 18 October, away at Levante, the club fell to its first defeat of the season, losing 1–0. The Blue-and-Whites fell to third in the table but were only a point off the new leaders, FC Cartagena. Griezmann was in the starting eleven once again. In the space of just a few weeks, he had gone from surprise guest to permanent fixture in the first team.

Chapter 13

How to Give a Whole City
its Smile Back

'This is a once-in-a-lifetime moment. We should enjoy every second.' Soaked to the skin, exhausted, with his white t-shirt drenched in water and the *ikurriña* (the flag of the Basque Country) across his shoulders, Antoine stops in front of a pack of journalists. The young man's joy flows out of him. When asked by a reporter if he would like 'to spend the rest of his life in the first division,' he says 'Yes!' before disappearing down the dressing room tunnel.

This brief exchange with the press had been preceded by scenes of immense happiness, full of emotion, tears and embraces. After three years in purgatory in the second division, Real Sociedad were finally returning to Spanish football's elite. The general jubilation was marked by some powerful images: the long hug between Griezmann and Lasarte, the shirt given by Antoine to the fans as a thank you for their unfailing support, and the chanting by a chorus of 32,000 spectators in the stands, not to mention the 10,000 others following the match on a giant screen set up near the stadium. The joy was felt by everyone and before beginning the traditional lap of honour, the players carried out a series of dives onto the Anoeta grass in front of the home end. Lasarte was thrown in the air by his men and the *txapela* (Basque beret) made an appearance, as did the

Peñarol flag, waved by Carlos Bueno. The manager then implored the fans and the club to 'remain united because together you can accomplish great things.' Lasarte went on to dedicate the moment to his father, originally from Andoín in the Gipuzkoa province of the Basque Country. In the midst of the general commotion, Antoine also took the time to pay his own tribute 'to the supporters, to the whole of San Sebastián and to my parents who watched the game on TV and are over the moon.'

It was time for the festivities. A platform was quickly set up in the middle of the grass and the euphoria spread throughout the stadium as the players and staff returned to the pitch. One by one, they came out of the Anoeta tunnel, running, jumping, some even doing backflips, as their names were read out by the announcer before being chanted and cheered by the fans. They were all wearing blue shirts with the slogan *'Lortu Dugu! Eskerrik asko!'* printed in white letters (We did it! A huge thank you!).

The young French player, still with the *ikurriña* around his neck, climbed onto the platform and led the crowd in a rendition of *'Campeónes! Campeónes! Olé! Olé! Olé!'*

Antoine was the warm-up act, while his partner in crime, Emilio Nsue, started singing a somewhat suspect version of the Real Sociedad anthem. The fireworks marked a wonderful end to the night of 13 June 2010, which would linger long in the memories of the *txuri urdin* supporters. The club had just officially confirmed its promotion to La Liga at the end of the 41st and penultimate match of the league season with a 2–0 win over Celta Vigo.

During the first half the home team were extremely nervous and Celta looked dangerous, coming closest with a Michu striker that hit the crossbar. Real struggled until Xavi Prieto opened the scoring with a penalty in the 50th minute after Griezmann was fouled in the area. Keen to share his delight with the fans, the captain of the Basque club injured himself as he tried to jump over the advertising hoardings dividing the pitch from the athletics track. He had to leave the field and did not reappear until the celebrations, with the help of a pair of crutches. Shortly after, in the 63rd minute, Antoine laid the ball off perfectly with his head to Carlos Bueno to make it 2–0 and that's how it remained until Teixeira Vitienes blew the final whistle to a deafening uproar.

The city of San Sebastián, which had been decorated in white and blue since dawn that morning, had become a scene of celebration. Despite the rain and 17°C temperatures, fans were swimming in the fountain in Plaza Pio II, while others celebrated on the Concha beach and yet more toasted the victory in the city's bars and inns until the early hours. The party continued the following day. Thousands of people crowded the route taken by a double-decker bus carrying the team to the Town Hall and then to the Gipuzkoa Provincial Council building. A huge crowd gathered in the Alderdi Eder gardens and the players were cheered as they appeared on the Town Hall balcony. The chanting began again, with refrains of *'Gora Erreala!'* (Long Live Real!) over and over again. Flags fluttered in the air and were being waved as far as the eye could see. Griezmann was the uncontested king of the party. The impression left by his appearance on the Town Hall balcony was confirmed when the players came down to the forecourt. Sporting various club scarves and a flag wrapped around his official Real tracksuit, he coaxed his teammates, even the most reluctant, into starting a conga. The soundtrack to this was provided by a throng of young fans who had already made him their idol.

For the first time in three years, San Sebastián was happy again and Griezmann had plenty to do with that. With his carefree attitude and youth, he had given the whole city its smile back. Even today, fans and journalists alike will tell you that the radical change of course embarked upon by the club began with the emergence of the young Frenchman.

The Burgundian had been the great revelation of the season, conquering the world like a breath of fresh air with his goals and celebrations. 'This was really something new for the home supporters. Usually, local players always made the same gesture, pumping their fists in the air and shouting ... nothing more. It had become a bit boring,' one fan admitted. Then Griezmann changed the rules.

Everyone still remembers 9 January 2010. In the 19th match of the league season, Real Sociedad were at home to Cádiz. In the 90th minute, the *txuri urdin* were leading 3–1 when suddenly, Antoine picked up the ball in the midfield, sped down the right wing, broke into the box and fired a shot in over Kiko Casilla's head. To celebrate his fifth goal in the second division, he dived into a mountain of snow piled up at the edge of the pitch as if he were jumping into a swimming pool. 'He wanted to do something funny,' remembers Lasarte, with a smile, 'but I think he hurt himself because the snow was really hard, almost frozen solid. Antoine was always coming up with something.' Griezmann had always enjoyed watching the celebrations of great champions on the television. When he was a child, he had dreamed of being able to take his turn at celebrating a goal. The dream had become a reality.

'Antoine looked like an angel but appearances can be deceptive. He was smart and a quick learner,' explained Lasarte, before adding: 'One of those who taught him the most was [his teammate] Carlos Bueno. He always had this image of being "*loco*" [crazy], someone who constantly gave the impression of fighting with himself but who knew how to give good advice and was capable of explaining the very essence of football perfectly. I think he was very important to Antoine. They're still good friends.'

'I just tried to explain to him what the future is like for a professional footballer, that it depends on you and what you have to do for your own career … just things like that, nothing more,' says Bueno, playing it down despite having seen it all during his career with different clubs around the world. He had begun at Peñarol, in Montevideo, before playing for PSG, Benfica, Sporting Lisbon, Boca Juniors and now, at the age of 37, the Santa Tecla Fútbol Club in San Salvador.

'Every day after training', remembers the Uruguayan striker, 'and even if Martín [Lasarte] didn't want us to – at least that was what he said in public – we would stay on the pitch for an extra hour. We would work on crosses, over and over, headers, free kicks and finishing. I was delighted to do it, to help Antoine learn new things that would be useful. He was a boy who lived and breathed football, playing matches at a hundred miles an hour, and he learned at a crazy speed. I like to tell myself that I taught him how to improve his relaxation, to hang in the air, to anticipate the movement of his opponent, to use his arms and his body to help him jump. Although I'm not particularly tall, my statistics for headed goals are good. I used to say to Antoine, I really insisted on it: size doesn't matter.'

'The pair got on well and the extra hours they spent training together bore fruit. I remember the match against Cádiz [5 June 2010] at the Carranza, which put us directly in contention for the title. Bueno scored a hat trick and Antoine delivered all three assists; they were perfect. It also worked in the opposite direction. Now, whenever I see Antoine score with his head, I always think of Bueno,' confirms Lasarte. 'They had the same gestures and ways of using their bodies.

But Carlitos did not just teach him how to jump, he also taught him the tricks of the trade: when to allow yourself to be brought down in the box, how to behave with opposition defenders.'

He also taught him about South American football, something that is still a passion of Antoine's. 'We would watch Peñarol games online. I wanted to get him to understand what the experience of football is like in Uruguay, because he's French and the atmosphere is a bit more subdued there than it is where I come from. We really had some great times together that year.' Carlos Bueno was, along with Martín Lasarte, the first to bring out Antoine's 'Uruguayan' side. It would soon be the turn of Diego Ifrán, a striker from the Cerro Chato who signed for Real in the summer of 2010, then of Chori Castro, who joined the *txuri urdin* during the 2012–13 season, before the Uruguayans of Atlético Madrid took over: 'Cebolla' Rodríguez, José María Giménez, Diego Godín and Óscar Ortega, known as El Profe (The Professor). Even now at France team gatherings, Antoine always takes with him a thermos containing an infusion of yerba maté leaves (a South American beverage).

But it was not just football from the southern hemisphere that fascinated the boy from Mâcon. 'Antoine was one of those who loved to listen to the stories Bueno, Bravo and I would tell,' explains Diego Rivas. 'Anecdotes about Boca, Sporting, Colo-Colo, Atlético and the fans at the Calderón. We told him we would teach him all the worst things about football and that he would discover the best things for himself. By the end of the season he had learned a lot: he was no longer the shy boy who had stayed out on the balcony in Tenerife. He was a nice kid, cheerful, always ready to have fun and joke around,' remembers Diego Rivas.

Antoine Griezmann's evolution was impressive. The

changes in his life were happening at an incredible speed and were sometimes difficult to handle. In the space of just a few months, he had gone from a complete unknown to a player in Real Sociedad's starting eleven. He had become the darling of the supporters; everyone was talking about him and they had nicknamed him 'Superantoine', 'Fabuloso', 'El Mago' (The Magician) or 'El ángel caído del cielo' (The Angel Fallen from the Sky). Europe's major clubs had begun watching him closely. Olympique Lyonnais and Girondins de Bordeaux had expressed their interest, as had the coach of the French Under-19 team. Antoine moved from Bayonne to San Sebastián, releasing himself from Éric Olhats's protection. He went to live with Carlos Bueno before renting with Emilio Nsue, who was two years older and shared his passion for the PlayStation, before getting his own apartment near the city centre. The boy was beginning to enjoy the pleasures of life. He spent his time with the team's other foreign players, with whom he would go out for lunch and dinner, dancing and having fun; these included Bueno, Nsue, Estrada and Alberto De La Bella, a Catalan who had arrived from Sevilla. It was not so easy to go out with the Basque members of the squad; with family, fiancées and friends nearby they were more closely watched than the foreign players in a city where the night-life was frankly not that highly regarded. San Sebastián only came alive at the end of the week and there were only so many nightclubs, pubs, bars and house parties. It was nothing like Madrid or Barcelona, where there are limitless distractions for young, well-known footballers. It is also important to note that San Sebastián is a small city: it is easy to bump into people here and there, and a small blond boy with blue eyes, wearing Real colours, was easy to spot. Every time he went out it was noticed, talked about in detail and exaggerated.

'At one point, stories were always doing the rounds about Antoine's frequent outings to such and such a place. What did I think about it? I thought that he was a nineteen-year-old kid who was doing the same thing other young people his age do. I just told him to be careful, to choose the days he went out wisely, wait for the right time and not to let things get out of hand. We tried to protect him,' explains Lasarte. 'That was what Alain, his father and Éric Olhats had asked us to do. They had asked us to look out for him. Sometimes I invited him over for dinner. I remember showing him some of my matches, when I was playing in the Copa Libertadores. We would talk about football, about what the stadiums and the game were like back then. I'm sure he was bored but it was a way of keeping an eye on him, of helping him adapt better to the changes in his life and to make sure that the fame did not go to his head. But it wasn't easy because sometimes Antoine would lose his battle with himself. Then he needed to be reprimanded, reasoned with and threatened, telling him that if he carried on like that, he would eventually end up on the bench or in the stands. But I have to say that, apart from in exceptional cases, Antoine always responded very well; he always listened to what we were saying and learned from it.'

Part father, part manager, Martín Lasarte tried to correct the boy's indolence and nurture the flashes of genius. Aranburu, Labaka, Prieto and especially Claudio Bravo gave him a hand. Whenever things went wrong, the Chilean goalkeeper would take the French player to one side and explain to him that if he wanted to become a professional footballer and stay at the top, he would have to improve his behaviour. Like the team's senior players and its manager, the club also played an important role in protecting its new phenomenon. It kept him as far as possible from the media, controlled his communication and emphasised that Antoine was still a training academy player. An anecdote remembered by Lasarte demonstrates this clearly: 'Every December, Real Sociedad gave its fans a team poster. It was a tradition and an important event in the life of the club. We were all kept informed about the day and time the photo would be taken; we were all supposed to shave and be presentable for the occasion. I looked down the list of players who would be in the picture but Antoine's name did not appear. I asked the technical director why and he told me that Griezmann did not play for the first team but for the reserves. I asked him what he meant by that. He had already played twelve matches with us, been very successful and become one of Real's figureheads but he wouldn't appear in the team photo? I understood that the club wanted to make sure he didn't get big headed, but Antoine [...] had come a long way in five months and earned the right to be in the photo.'

In the end he did appear, with a smile on his face, in the front row, to the left of Carlos Bueno and to the right of the three keepers. Four months after he appeared in the team photo he signed his first professional contract. 'I remember that to start with he was worried because he had to play at least ten games with the first team to land it.' Diego Rivas recalls: 'As a laugh, Claudio Bravo and I told him that if he wanted to play the ten games and then sign a professional contract, he had to obey us and do everything we told him. And, of course, he did.'

*

On 18 April 2010, an announcement appeared on the club's website: 'Real Sociedad and Antoine Griezmann have reached an agreement that will keep the player at the club for a total duration of six years until 30 June 2015. His integration into the first team prompted the club to review its conditions.'

The statement was accompanied by a photo of the handshake between Antoine, dressed from head to toe in black, and Jokin Aperribay, the club president. There was also the statement issued by the director of football, Loren: 'Griezmann is one of the players around whom we would like to build the future of Real. He has enormous potential and is progressing rapidly. We are proud that he wants to continue improving at the club.' When asked by journalists about his short-term plans, Antoine answered that he would do everything within his power to help the club win promotion to the first division and to write his name into the history of Real, alongside Darko Kovačević, Nihat and Valeri Karpin, the club's latest idols.

The first objective was achieved on 13 June 2010. The second did not take long to become a reality.

Chapter 14

Fond Memories of France

The surprises just kept on coming for Antoine. There was barely time to savour his first year in the first team, marked by promotion to La Liga, when a new challenge presented itself: the Under-19 European Championships with the France team, played at home, in Normandy, in July 2010.

Antoine's return to Les Bleus' fold came about thanks to one man: Peïo Sarratia. The man, now in his sixties, was an iconic figure in Basque football: ten years volunteering at the Ustaritz and Arin Luzien clubs and thirty years in the service of the districts and the Aquitaine League, where he saw out the end of his career as regional technical adviser. Since leaving the French Football Federation in 2011, he has moved to Uruguay. More precisely to Montevideo, where he fell in love with the country and continues to live out his passion for football today.

Sarratia has had very little direct contact with Antoine but, in small ways, has influenced his career. Sarratia began following him as soon as he arrived in the Basque Country. His friend and French Football Federation colleague, Paul Guérin, told him about the boy's recruitment in 2005. At the time, he lobbied for the new recruit to join the ranks of the sports students at the private Saint-Bernard School in Bayonne but it was not to the liking of some of the French Federation directors. 'It was the subject of several meetings at the national technical centre at Clairefontaine. I was told that young people nurtured by foreign clubs could not take advantage of these sports programmes in France. I thought it was ridiculous and in the end we had to give up.'

Late July 2009. Peïo Sarratia's path once again crossed indirectly with that of the young striker. The regional technical adviser for the Pyrénées-Atlantiques visited his Spanish neighbour to attend a footballing conference. There he met the new Real Sociedad manager, Martín Lasarte, in the reception hall: 'He immediately told me about Antoine. He had had him train with the professional squad for the first time that very morning.'

Over the following weeks, Sarratia used his network of contacts to get information from far and wide with the aim of telling the French directors about the player as soon as possible: 'I called Paul Guérin, who had followed Antoine's early years at Mâcon. I also contacted the man who had discovered him, his mentor Éric Olhats. There was no time to lose because Antoine had just made his official debut as a professional and there were already rumours that the Spanish federation might be interested in picking him.'

Peïo Sarratia spoke directly to Francis Smerecki, head of the France Under-19 team: 'I insisted that he take him' says Peïo Sarratia. 'But Éric Olhats told me to calm down. He didn't want Antoine to start thinking about national team selection too soon. Smerecki did eventually call him up though.' The French manager did not really have any choice: Antoine Griezmann was running amok in the Spanish second division. When he was not scoring, he was providing assists. So it was that in early March 2010, he was called up by his country for the first time for two friendlies against the Ukraine that were part of the final phase of preparation for the Under-19 European Championships.

For the Griezmann clan, if it was not revenge it certainly

looked a little like it. Snubbed by the French training academies five years earlier, Real Sociedad's phenomenon was preparing to join the elite of the 1991 generation. 'It was nevertheless a real jibe at the French Federation, which had never given him anything. It was also a real reward for all the sacrifices made by the family. He had left for Real Sociedad by the back door and was coming back to his country with the label of a Spaniard,' says an insider.

Antoine kept these thoughts to himself. His journey had taught him humility. He also knew that despite his recent experience in the Spanish second division, he would have plenty to do to claim his place in the France team. Competition among the 1991 generation was fierce: two years earlier, in Turkey, they had lost in the Euro U17 final to Spain (4–0). There was plenty of talent and strong personalities in the team populated by potential stars. These included the promising captain Gueïda Fofana (Le Havre) and Cédric Bakambu (FC Sochaux); those based in England, with the phenomenon Gaël Kakuta (Chelsea), Francis Coquelin and Gilles Sunu (both Arsenal), and Chris Mavinga (Liverpool); not to mention the Lyonnais gang, with its six players Sébastien Faure, Timothée Kolodziejczak, Clément Grenier, Enzo Reale, Yannis Tafer and Alex Lacazette.

It was with his former neighbours from Olympique Lyonnais that Antoine naturally made first contact: 'On the first day of training, he was on tenterhooks. It wasn't easy for him to join a group that had already made the final of the U17 Euros,' remembers Sébastien Faure (formerly of OL and Glasgow Rangers). 'Smerecki had his favourites and the squad had barely changed in two years. We knew that Antoine had played regularly in the Spanish second division, but not much more than that. He was unknown to most of the players on the team, except Clément [Grenier] and Alex

[Lacazette], who immediately recognised him. They knew he was the one who had come to Lyon for a trial when he was thirteen. They also remembered playing against him in a friendly in Mâcon.' The hours spent on the pitch during his trial at the Plaine des Jeux de Gerland in Lyon had not been in vain after all: at least they helped ease his integration into the France team.

At dinner time, 'The Spaniard' was already surrounded and at his ease when his teammates began to tap their knives against their glasses. At the next table, Francis Smerecki's staff offered approving smiles. It was time for his initiation: a classic in football for any new player joining a team. 'Sing, sing, sing!' the group chanted in unison.

Antoine must have been a little embarrassed but he did not flinch. The Real Sociedad striker got up from his chair and turned to face his teammates. Quick as a flash, he started singing *La Bamba*: a classic and a guaranteed crowd-pleaser! There was laughing, whistling and clapping. This was the mischievous kid, the king of pranks. Of course, his performance was a long way from that of Ritchie Valens in the late 1950s but his cover of *La Bamba* had helped Grizou score points. Now he just had to prove himself on the pitch.

The first match against the Ukraine would take place on 2 March 2010 near Orléans, at Saint-Jean-de-Braye. A small crowd gathered at the Petit Bois complex to see Antoine Griezmann's first outing in a blue shirt. He started up front alongside Gilles Sunu and Yannis Tafer. Smerecki wanted to give himself time to see his new player. Antoine had 90 minutes to show what he could do. 'You could see immediately that he was comfortable,' says the central defender Sébastien Faure. 'He brought something different, a technical basis that was different to ours.' His first touches were good, as were his combinations with Tafer and Sunu. He immediately developed a technical relationship with the midfielders Kakuta, Grenier and Coquelin. Antoine gave his all. He was generous as usual. The match ended without a goal but Smerecki had fallen under Antoine's spell: 'He really added something to the team, an extra technical touch with his left foot. I didn't need to explain things ten times to Antoine. He was already very mature and you could sense there was great room for progression.'

Two days later it was déjà-vu: the mini-Bleus met the Ukraine Under-19 team for a second time just a few kilometres away at the Crébezeaux stadium in Saint-Denis de l'Hôtel. Smerecki logically rotated his team and changed his strike force completely. Reale, Lacazette and Bakambu started; Tafer, Sunu and Griezmann were on the bench. The score was 1–1 when Antoine came on in the 69th minute, replacing Lacazette, who had just equalised.

Antoine had about twenty minutes to convince his manager once and for all. Calling for the ball in space, throw-ins, playing back in defence. There was no limit to Antoine's effort. Space up front was at a premium thanks to a tight and athletic defence, at least until the 88th minute. Antoine picked up the ball in a seemingly innocuous position, wound up his left foot and fired a shot right into the centre of the goal, completely surprising Levchenko, the young Ukrainian keeper. Goal! It was Antoine's first for France. His teammates rushed over to congratulate him. He had passed his first test with Les Bleus. The doors of the Under-19 European Championships were wide open for him.

By the time he joined up with the squad in July 2010 to prepare for the Under-19 Euros the landscape of French football had changed somewhat. France had just experienced a catastrophic June, which culminated in the player revolt at an open training session is Knysna. The team's elimination in the first round of the World Cup in South Africa, and in particular the lamentable behaviour of Raymond Domenech's team, who famously went on strike, had tarnished the image of French football. The Federation was expecting a lot from the Under-19 Euros on home soil, hoping they would go some way to restoring the Tricolore's reputation and to sending some signs of hope for a changing of the guard.

Like his teammates, Antoine had watched his TV sadly and helplessly as his elders struggled against Uruguay, Mexico and South Africa. He was aware of the added dimension the Under-19 European Championships had taken on. He also knew that he now had a reputation to keep up and a role to play in the competition, because, unlike many of his France teammates who were still vegetating in the reserve team, he had just played a full season as a professional.

'By the time we came together for the Euros, he was already a big part of the team,' confirms Sébastien Faure. 'Everyone liked him. He had his head screwed on and did not put on any airs and graces. You could talk to him about all sorts of different subjects, not just football.' During the tough training sessions, his teammates discovered his true character: 'He loved to laugh and joke around with Lacazette, Kakuta and Nego. He had a different mentality to us. He even celebrated his goals in training. We couldn't get over it, it was really funny!' reports the attacking midfielder, Enzo Reale (formerly of OL and Lorient).

Antoine was in Francis Smerecki's starting eleven for the first two group matches: 4–1 and 5–0 wins over the Netherlands and Austria respectively. Although he was quiet against the Oranje, he scored twice against Austria, firstly to make it 1–0 in the 19th minute and then to make it 3–0 at the start of the last fifteen minutes, with a piece of skill that got the fans out of their seats in the small Hazé stadium. 'It was a magnificent move,' recalls Enzo Reale, who also scored during the game. 'It began with a cross from Chris Mavinga, on the end of which Antoine produced a stunning left-footed half volley. In just a handful of matches he had already become indispensable to the team.'

France held their own in their group, finishing with a 0–0 draw against England (in which Antoine played fifteen minutes). The team met Croatia in the semi-final in a game that went down to the wire. Antoine was all over the pitch, leaping on Cédric Bakambu when the Sochaux player scored the winning goal in the 83rd minute. 2–1 and Les Bleus were in the final. The pleasure was two-fold as there they would play Spain, who had humiliated them two years earlier during the U17 Euros.

30 July 2010. The Stade Michel d'Ornano, where Stade Malherbe de Caen play their home games, was packed to the rafters with 21,000 spectators, a number never before seen in France for an Under-19 match. Those watching from the stands included the players' friends and family, representatives of French football and the President of UEFA, Michel Platini, who had come to present the trophy and admire the two teams he had heard so much about.

For France, Smerecki had once again decided to place his trust in Antoine Griezmann, who started on the left wing in a strike force that included Gilles Sunu on the right, Cédric Bakambu up front and Gaël Kakuta in support. The Lyonnais players Tafer and Lacazette would start on the bench.

France versus Spain was, of course, the best possible match-up for Antoine. He knew almost all the opposing players as he had played against them in Spanish youth leagues. The team picked by Luis Milla did not include any of his Real Sociedad teammates. There were, however, two neighbouring Basques from Athletic Bilbao who would start on the bench (Aitor Fernández and Iker Muniain). There was a whole host of players from Barça (Marc Bartra, Oriol Romeu, Martin Montoya and Thiago Alcantara), Koke, his future partner at Atlético Madrid, and Sergio Canales, the formidable playmaker for Racing Santander recruited the following season by Real Madrid.

How did Antoine fit into all of that? As the 'French-Spaniard' would he be able to handle an event that was so special? Would he be overcome with emotion when the Stade d'Ornano rang out to the sound of *La Marseillaise*? Had he already played out the final in his mind? Was he focusing too much on doing well? Or was he simply having an off day? During the first 45 minutes of the final, it was hard to recognise the number 7 who had brought so much freshness to Les Bleus in recent weeks. Like his teammates, he seemed lost on the pitch. Unable to make the right choices, over-whelmed, jostled, helpless in the face of the *toque*, the short passing game instigated by the *Roja*. At half time, it came as no surprise that Spain were in front. They were leading 1–0 after an unstoppable cross from the Real Madrid number 9, Rodrigo, in the eighteenth minute.

Antoine's head was down as he returned to the dressing room. He seemed very upset as he started down the tunnel. Fifteen minutes later he failed to reappear on the pitch. Was this his manager's choice? Apparently not. His ankle was troubling him too much. He was replaced by another left-footed player, Yannis Tafer. That was where the Euros ended for him. Or at least where it should have ended.

Despite the pain and disappointment, Antoine quickly refocused on the team's goal and their chance to win a first international title. From the bench, his level of investment in the game was at 100 per cent; he leapt up from the bench on three occasions. The first, in the 49th minute when his replacement, Yannis Tafer, sent Gilles Sunu through perfectly into space to equalise, 1–1. The second, in the 85th minute when the stadium started shaking after a throw-in from Kakuta was headed towards the far post by Lacazette. 'GOOOOOOAAAAAAAAAAL!' shouted the announcer in a stadium blanketed by waving red, white and blue flags. Finally, Antoine sprang up again when, after injury time, the final whistle was blown by the referee Stefan Struder. 'Champions of Europe!' the young French players shouted at the tops of their voices.

With his flip-flops and injured ankle, Antoine was the last to join the mêlée of players that had formed near a corner post. He was struggling to hold back his tears. Too many emotions. Joy. Frustration? A few months ago, he had been the forgotten man of French football. Here he was, an Under-19 European champion and, alongside the others of the 1991 generation, a new standard-bearer for French football. 'This team is a breath of fresh air for football in this country,' Frédéric Thiriez said live into the TV cameras. 'The Bleuets are the future of Les Bleus. They've demonstrated a desire and collective spirit that are the ingredients of success.' In a corner of the pitch, the future star of French football was savouring his first international title: 'It was magnificent. I'm so proud to wear the colours of my country. We've got a great team. It's been so much fun!'

Chapter 15

Celebrations

Antoine had played more than fifty games for his club and national team. He had even won the Under-19 European Championships. Real Sociedad quite rightly thought he deserved an extra two weeks rest. Antoine Griezmann thought otherwise and, on 11 August, he called Martín Lasarte to ask him to shorten his holiday. He had already had one week of doing nothing. 'I wanted to stay with the squad,' explains Antoine, who assured his manager that the week's holiday spent with his family in Tunisia had been enough to recharge his batteries. He was eager to get back to playing, particularly in La Liga. It was a childhood dream that was now within reach. He would finally be able to see how he measured up against Messi and Ronaldo, to test his true level against the stars of Spanish football. He would also be able to walk out onto the greatest pitches in La Liga; the Bernabéu, Camp Nou. As far as he was concerned, there was no time to lose and he wanted to join back up with the squad as soon as possible for the pre-season matches; the technical staff drew up a tailor-made programme to get him back to where he needed to be after a challenging first season as a professional. A number of players had left Lasarte's squad: Carlos Bueno, Emilio Nsue and Jonathan Estrada. Bueno, his Uruguayan friend, who would have liked to have stayed with the Blue-and-Whites, had signed for Universidad de Chile on 8 August, before joining the Mexican club Querétaro

FC five months later. Nsue, who had taken Antoine into his home and always seen him as a little brother, went back to Mallorca. Estrada, a first eleven player on the left wing before losing his place to Griezmann, had gone back to live in Bogotá to play for Millonarios. Departures were matched by arrivals: the Basque player Joseba Llorente, a very experienced and tough centre forward, returned to Real Sociedad after a stint at Villareal. At €2.5 million it was the biggest signing of the summer for the San Sebastián club. Paco Sutil, a promising left-footed midfielder, joined from Eibar, while Raúl Tamudo, another good striker, was bought from Espanyol, and Diego Ifrán arrived from Danubio in Montevideo. In other words, competition for the forward positions was fierce but this was of no particular concern to Antoine: 'The more competition there is, the better I play,' he declared with all the bravado of his nineteen years. As for his new-found fame in France in the wake of the Under-19 European Championship title, he asserted: 'I have to keep my feet on the ground and continue to work hard. I know there are going to be difficult times but I need to make sure I don't lose my head.'

Speaking of France, the Union de Football Mâconnais, the club where Antoine had cut his teeth as a footballer, were knocking on Real Sociedad's door. They were asking the Basque club for €165,000 in training rights for the years he spent playing in Saône-et-Loire from aged six to aged fourteen. This was a legitimate request under FIFA rules. The San Sebastián club fired back that the payment would only be made once Griezmann's status in the professional team had been confirmed. According to Real Sociedad's lawyers, the French number 27 had still been playing as an 'amateur' the previous season. This year things had changed. Antoine had taken the number 7, the same as David Beckham, the player he had always admired for his natural class, which he tried to imitate, from his haircut to his tattoos, from his extravagant look to the long-sleeved shirts he wore during matches. The Frenchman had a new number and plenty of expectation on his shoulders as the new season dawned. 'I hope to play well to help Real win matches and stay in the first division. They deserve to be there. The fans have been waiting for three years for us to go back up and I think they'll do everything they can to support us this season,' Antoine told the *Diario Vasco*. He added: 'They're even shouting "Aupa Griezmann!" [Come on Griezmann!] at me in the street.'

The La Liga season started on 29 August 2010. Real faced Villareal at the Anoeta. The new number 7 started on the substitutes' bench. This was not a managerial whim, the Frenchman was simply lacking in fitness. He came on for Paco Sutil in the 61st minute. His debut in the Spanish first division was something that had motivated him since his arrival at the Zubieta. Real Sociedad's big return to La Liga went very well indeed. They beat the 'Yellow Submarine' 1–0, making the dreams of the 24,865 spectators in the Anoeta come true.

'I've got a funny anecdote about that game,' explains Martín Lasarte. 'Villareal had a hard, tough defender whose name I've forgotten. I had told Antoine about what opponents did to me when I was a player and what annoyed me most as a central defender. If he brings you down or commits too many fouls on you, I told him, pick a tuft of grass and throw it at him. The kid remembered and did exactly what I'd told him after the first foul. The Villareal defender wanted to kill him!'

Antoine had to be content with coming on towards the end of the next few games. He was still not yet in top form. It was not until 18 September that Lasarte gave him a place in the starting eleven, against José Mourinho's Real Madrid at home. The *txuri urdin* dominated, putting Madrid under pressure and clearly deserving a point. But at the end of the match, a deflected free kick from Cristiano Ronaldo gifted the Special One's team all three points. It was a blow to the San Sebastián team and heralded a series of disappointments against Osasuna, Mallorca and Levante.

On 25 October, the club could finally take some heart from a win marked by Antoine's first goal in La Liga and an unforgettable celebration. Real were playing Deportivo de La Coruña at the Anoeta in a duel between two teams looking for points to stay up. The match was not particularly thrilling. If truth be told, it was pretty dull. The San Sebastián players had possession of the ball but seemed unable to do anything dangerous until Llorente finally found a way through with a header in the 17th minute on the end of a great cross from Alberto De La Bella. Despite the early goal, there was little to write home about in the first 45 minutes. Fortunately, the situation changed for the better at the start of the second half. Deportivo reacted and, to avoid an equaliser, Claudio Bravo had to pull off a decisive save following a volley from Riki. Antoine stepped up in the wake of this warning. After ghosting through recent matches, he finally resurfaced. On the end of a cross from Carlos Martínez, he unleashed a volley that Aranzubia struggled to parry. Then, in the 70th minute, he scored. Xabi Prieto swapped places with Martínez and moved to the right, before measuring a cross right into the middle of the box. Antoine jumped up, found himself in space in front of a defender and his teammate Llorente and, with all the anger that had built up over recent weeks, fired the ball into the back of the net. He ran to the corner post, waved to his teammates, jumped over the advertising hoardings, crossed the athletics track and got into the driving seat of the Opel parked in the area reserved for Real's sponsors. Pretending to drive off, he was joined by his acolytes Xabi Prieto, Gorka Elustondo and Alberto De La Bella.

'I'm the happiest kid in the world!' Antoine confessed in the post-match interview. 'I'd been preparing that celebration for a while. I'd asked them to open the car doors and told my teammates to join me.' The quirky celebration earned him a yellow card but he didn't care. Yet again the French player had surprised everyone. He broke with traditional local codes of restraint 'to invent a celebration the like of which no one has ever seen before,' confirmed the Gol TV commentators. He had no qualms about using the media to get himself noticed. He knew that Burger King had launched a competition to reward the most original celebration that season. 'We talked about it,' Antoine admitted, 'and we thought we could win. I hope we'll have other opportunities to surprise people.'

He was already attracting the attention of some of the biggest clubs in Europe. Jokin Aperribay was forced to deny rumours of his departure, including those that claimed Antoine was on his way to Liverpool for €8.5 million. 'We have not received any offers,' confirmed the president on 18 November. 'Antoine has no intention of leaving, whether in January or June.' The player himself confirmed this for the Radio Marca microphones: 'I'm happy at Real. I hope to stay here for many years.' He did, however, confess to the journalists that the interest from Liverpool was real and that Sevilla were also keeping watch.

Amid the transfer rumours and nondescript performances loomed the Basque derby against Athletic Bilbao, the first after three years of waiting. It is a unique showdown, unparalleled anywhere in the world; despite the fierce rivalry, the match is seen first and foremost as a celebration of the Basque Country. This time it would also be a derby between Llorente (Fernando) and Llorente (Joseba), Bravo and Iraizoz, Antoine and Iker (Muniain), the two revelations. Everyone was expecting Real to struggle because they had just been promoted to the top division. But this would not be the case. On 5 December 2010, the Blue-and-Whites beat the Leones 2–0 with surprising ease thanks to a penalty converted by Prieto and an own goal from San José. Griezmann came very close to scoring the goal of the game: after pinching the ball out of Iraizoz's hands with his head, he saw his shot come back off the post as the goal gaped. It was a real missed opportunity but one that did not prevent him being invited the following day onto *'Uyyyy'*, the *ETB* programme presented by Óscar Terol.

It was the first time the new star of the *txuri urdin* had found himself on a television set and he handled it well. They looked back at his goals, haircuts and celebrations. The latest had taken place after his third goal in La Liga against Hércules, in which, wearing a green shirt, he posed as an archer as he slid along the grass on his knees. This mime had already been tried by Kiko, the Atlético Madrid striker and copied by 'El Niño', Fernando Torres. Griezmann held his ground rather well opposite the presenter, who had assistants and comedians to call on for support. He also showed a certain amount of skill when asked to repeat a few words in Basque. The audience was won over and went into noisy raptures at each of his responses, reminiscent of Beatles fans during the 1960s.

In all the excitement, Antoine also had the chance to look back over his meteoric rise. He said that his father, Martín Lasarte and his coaches at the academy had warned him endlessly about the demands and level required to play in La Liga, where games are faster and more technical. He was not necessarily surprised by how easy he found it to adapt: 'My father and uncles told me that this is how things can be in football.' Nor did he seem surprised by the start his team had made to the season, currently resulting in talk of a European Cup spot. 'Why shouldn't Real Sociedad be able to play in Europe next season?' he asked.

Unfortunately, the success of the derby and his first television appearance were followed by a thrashing. At Camp Nou, Barça, who had just put five past Real Madrid, inflicted the same on Griezmann's Real Sociedad. It was the first in a series of four consecutive defeats, the rest coming against Valencia, Zaragoza and Sevilla. The Basques did not regain their footing until 15 January, in an away match at the Coliseum Alfonso Pérez. They scored four times against Getafe. The second came in the 32nd minute when, latching onto a cross from Llorente, Antoine scored with a stunning volley from inside the box, sending the ball over Jordi Codina's head. The Burgundian player celebrated his goal by kissing the *ikurriña*, the Basque flag sewn onto the left sleeve of his green shirt. He did this right under the nose of the stand occupied by the Getafe ultras, the Comandos Azules. It was something he would soon live to regret as he was whistled and booed for the remaining 68 minutes. As soon as the ball came anywhere near him, he was jeered. The fans were not the only ones to lay into him. Even the opposing captain, Manu del Moral, asked him to explain himself. His teammates Diego Rivas and Xabi Prieto got involved and an altercation almost broke out with Pedro Rodriguez, a Getafe physio. Lasarte tried to calm things down during the post-match press conference: 'He made a mistake by celebrating his goal in this way, but he's young and sometime these things happen.' In the end, Antoine was forced to apologise: 'I didn't think the celebration would provoke such a reaction. I would like to say sorry even if I did it innocently. When I score, I behave like a child.'

But just how could such a gesture stir up so much anger, provoke the wrath of the crowd and almost lead to a political debate? 'A few days earlier [on 8 January], the Basque members of the team [eight players, including the captain Mikel Aramburu] had signed a petition calling for the transfer of ETA militants to prisons in the Basque Country. Antoine kissed the *irrukiña* out of solidarity with his teammates,' explains Lasarte. 'He did it without really realising, unconsciously, but the Getafe supporters were waiting for something like that and some of the Madrid journalists turned it into something political, as if Griezmann was taking a stand on the issue. He had unwittingly got himself into quite a mess.'

Regardless of political and territorial matters, this victory against Getafe would remain the last by Real on their travels that season. From 15 January to May, Lasarte's team failed to win even a single point away from home, failing to capitalise on the strong foundation they had built up over the previous months. Real went from dreaming of a European place to fearing relegation at the end of the season The *txuri urdin* escaped at the very last minute thanks to wins at home against Sporting Gijon, Zaragoza, Barcelona and a mutually beneficial draw with Getafe on the final day of the league season. On 21 May, the two sides were playing for survival at the Anoeta. In light of results at other grounds around Spain, a draw would guarantee survival in the top division for both the Basques and the Madrid-based team. The game finished with one goal each and celebrations all round. Real Sociedad ended the 2010–11 season in 15th place in a league won by Pep Guardiola's Barcelona ahead of José Mourinho's

Real Madrid. Antoine Griezmann had played 37 matches in La Liga and two in the Copa del Rey, with a total of seven goals. The last two had been scored against Sporting Gijon on 17 April 2011. Two goals and yet another stunt.

Imanol Martínez is a steward. He had been working at the Anoeta for four years. With his back to the game, he is required to keep a watchful eye on the public. He is forbidden from turning around, whatever the reason, and is paid not to. In the 78th minute that afternoon, just as he was looking straight ahead at the Peña Mujika supporters, he heard the rumble of the 25,000 people in the stand, screaming and celebrating the goal that made it 2–1. Just then he felt someone put their arm around his shoulder. 'What the hell is that?' he said to himself. He did not move a muscle, continued watching the terraces and doing his work, but nevertheless stole a glance to one side: it was Antoine Griezmann! Imanol Martínez could not believe his eyes. He stayed stock still. The Frenchman pointed to the fans and said 'Look at that!'

'It's really amazing!' was all the dumbfounded man had time to utter before Griezmann was knocked over by his teammates.

'After five defeats in a row, his two goals against Sporting Gijon were crucially important,' explains Lasarte. 'They allowed us to lift our heads and go into the home stretch of the season with a different state of mind. We won the next two games, making our fans particularly happy with a 2–1 win over Barça at the Anoeta. Then we made sure we'd stayed up.' Despite having achieved this objective and with a year still to run on his contract, it was not enough to guarantee Martín Lasarte his place in the dugout next season. On 25 May, four days after the end of the season, the Uruguayan was pushed out. There were many theories about his departure: some believe the problem came from a cooling of relations with Aperribay, others that it was the result of a disagreement over the non-extension of Diego Rivas's contract, or perhaps that the style of play favoured by the Uruguayan manager had convinced neither the president nor the director of football at the Basque club. One thing is sure, Lasarte was disappointed about how things ended, as well as about the timing of the announcement, but he remains satisfied by the things they achieved, the affection he received from the fans and the unfailing support of his players. Now back in Montevideo, he takes stock of his two years at Real Sociedad. He is also happy whenever Griezmann sends him his best, via Diego Godín, or whenever the French player says: 'Lasarte helped me grow.'

'I'm delighted, just as I am whenever Luis Suárez talks about me. Antoine and Luis are two players who had a lot in common when they were younger. They never hid behind their age to take risks. And they both knew very early on what they wanted to achieve. Luis wanted to play for Barcelona; Antoine told me that he would wear a France shirt at the World Cup. As far as I was concerned they were just the words of two eighteen-year-old kids. But look at them now.'

Chapter 16

Stay or Go

'I've made my decision. I want to go to Atlético Madrid because they compete regularly for European trophies. I want to progress and my dream is to play for France. Moving clubs is the best way to get there. Particularly because I'll be able to play with some great players at Atlético. I was supposed to extend my contract with Real Sociedad a few months ago but I haven't been offered anything. The directors have been promising me an increase for weeks and months now, telling me I'm important to the club. But nothing's materialised. I like the idea of going to Atlético Madrid. I hope the two clubs can come to an agreement soon.'

From Colombia, where he was playing with the Bleuets in the Under-20 World Cup, Griezmann issued a statement through the newspaper *L'Équipe* that he wanted to leave Real Sociedad. The French player made the declaration on 4 August 2011 and it did not find favour with the *txuri urdin* directors or supporters, to say the least. Loren, the director of football, responded via *Euskal Telebista* that this was unacceptable behaviour towards the club that had trained him. 'He doesn't need to go to such lengths to improve the conditions of his contract,' said Loren. He also warned the number 7: 'He needs to be careful because Atlético are using him to get something. In the offices of the Vicente Calderón, they're well aware that he won't leave for the sum they're offering.'

The 'Griezmann to Atlético' rumour was not new. The

story had been newspaper fodder for more than a month already. In early July, the Madrid club made an offer for the services of the young Frenchman that consisted of €7 million plus two players: 'Fran' Mérida, who trained at the Arsenal youth academy and had joined Atlético in 2010, as well as Raúl García, the former Osasuna midfielder who had played more than 100 matches for the *Colchoneros*. The offer was rejected by the Real board because the club had no need to bolster its coffers by selling its little gem. It was only prepared to deal with Atlético if they made a particularly tempting offer because Griezmann had a release clause of €30 million since extending his contract a year earlier. Miguel Ángel Gil Marín, the Atlético administrator, had had the French player in his sights for a long time. He saw him as the ideal replacement for Sergio Agüero, who had gone to Manchester City for €45 million. But he was not the only one targeting Real's number 7. There were rumours of interest from Pep Guardiola. He had contacted Antoine and Barça had also sounded out his representative, John Williams, but the approach by the Catalan club had been turned down. The Burgundian was aware of his value and was not keen on spending his time warming the substitutes' bench. 'I don't think I want to go to Barcelona,' he told *RMC*. 'If I did I would be fighting for my position with Villa and Pedro, but at Real I'm going to play regularly'.

Valencia, OL and OM also enquired about Real's price and intentions regarding the possible sale of their new star, but it was Atlético who proved to be the most insistent when they came back with a fresh offer of €10 million. It was even said that the Madrid team had already come to an agreement with the player for a five-year contract. Despite the Real directors' refusal to negotiate, Antoine once again publicly demonstrated his desire to leave. 'Atlético is an attractive club. It's one of Spain's biggest teams and they always play in the Champions or Europa Leagues. The fans are extraordinary and the stadium is almost full for every game. If I have to leave, that's where I'm going,' he told *Foot Mercato*. In late July, he told *Radio Euskadi*: 'I would like to play at Atlético alongside Forlán and Tiago. It would help me to become a better player.' And so it was until early August, when the player announced: 'I want to go to Atlético.' This assertion was quickly reversed. Real published a statement from Antoine on its official website on 4 August: 'I never said I wanted to go to Atlético, I simply said that any footballer would want to play alongside Diego Forlán, but that would also be the case alongside Messi, Benzema or Van Nistelrooy. That doesn't mean I want to leave. I want to stay here. The fans make me happy when they chant my name or whenever I see a kid in my shirt. Why would I want to leave when I have everything here? Real was the only club that would take a chance on me. My teammates, my manager, the fans – they all have faith in me and I feel wanted. I promised I would stay and I will.'

It was a very strange and sudden turnaround. Some put it down to the telling-off he had been given by the San Sebastián club. The directors told him not to insist because they would not give in. In short, he needed to be reasonable, at least for now. Order seemed to have been restored following the statement posted on the Basque club's website. Philippe Montanier who had taken over from Martín Lasarte on the Real bench, chose not to comment on the statements from his player. But when it came to assessing his first month in charge of the club, the former Valenciennes coach said: 'I'm sure of one thing, I'm counting on Antoine this season.' He also wished him luck with France in the Under-20 World Cup, claiming that a win 'would also be good for Real.'

On 25 August, after failing to bring home the World Cup
(the Bleuets finished fourth after a 2–0 semi-final defeat
against Portgual), Griezmann appeared at a press conference at the Zubieta to ask for forgiveness from Real's directors, his teammates and fans. He said he never wanted to
leave Real Sociedad. It may have been reported by more
than one journalist but it was not true. The only thing that
was true was that he wanted to play alongside La Liga's best
players. He spoke with Loren and assured him that Real
was the best club for him. It hurt him to be described as
mercenary. Even his sister, Maud, who knew nothing about
football, advised him to set the record straight, because he
was being badmouthed. 'The fans at the Anoeta can whistle
at me but I'll keep giving my best for Real, as I've always
done,' he promised. Antoine was right about one thing:
from his very first appearance, the *txuri urdin* fans showed
no mercy with their whistling. It was 3 September 2011, a
friendly game between Real Sociedad and Stade Brestois.
The stands were half empty but the fans who were there in
attendance made their displeasure with the French player
clear. The fans and ultras felt betrayed by the boy they had
put on a pedestal as their new idol, by this young man from
the training academy who, as soon as he had left the nest,
already wanted to fly away to distant lands, deserting the club
that had nurtured him.

The whistles from his fans hurt him, very much, but
Antoine knew that everything changes very quickly in football, from one Sunday to the next, and that even the most
extreme opinions are easily tempered. So much so that the
number 7's stock soon rose once more and he began to
regain the affections of the Real supporters. He scored the
goal to make it 2–2 at home against Barça in the second
match of the season, before narrowly missing out on giving

his team the lead in the Basque derby on 2 October when his strike ricocheted back off the post.

Unfortunately, Antoine would find himself regretting his statements once again. A new scandal broke out two days later in the calm of Clairefontaine, where the French Under-20 team were preparing for their Euro 2013 qualifying matches against Kazakhstan and Romania. Alban Lagoutte from *Football.fr* asked whether there was any basis to the summer's transfer rumours. Griezmann responded, 'Yes, there had been an official approach for me by *Los Colchoneros* during the U20 World Cup but nobody acted on it. After that, I got fed up and asked the club not to talk to me about it anymore because the press was constantly asking the same question and taking my answers out of context. I had had enough. Eventually, I ended up squashing all the rumours but I was still whistled at by the fans in the Anoeta during my first match of the season.'

Lagoutte probed further. 'In other words, will you have to leave Real Sociedad next summer for a bigger club?'

'I hope to be able to do that next summer, yes. I'm currently in discussions with my president about my release clause. It's set at €30 million, as it is for every player on the team. The aim is to lower it for me in June. I would like it if neither side had to lose out. They could sell me at a reasonable price, knowing, of course, that I'm not worth €30 million. It's too soon to talk about all that, but afterwards I would like to be able to leave, yes, but stay in La Liga because it is definitely a league that fits well with my football.'

The damage was done. Griezmann's response provoked Jokin Aperribay's anger. The Real Sociedad president raged on the pages of *Marca*: 'What Griezmann has to do is find his best level, express himself on the pitch and score goals. I haven't discussed a lowering of his release clause with him. That's not true. There is no agreement with Real. His agent did come to the club three times but we told him that Antoine's contract runs until 2015. Real will sell one of its players when it thinks it's the right time. We're currently thinking first and foremost about keeping the club in the first division and not "how much am I going to earn and at which club."'

Alain Griezmann responded to the president's statements in an interview with the *Mundo Deportivo*. He did not justify his son's comments but rather believed Antoine had made a mistake under the influence of his agent John Williams, and that he had been taken for a ride by certain journalists who knew how to get a twenty-year-old kid to say whatever they wanted. He told Antoine not to say anything else and to let his football do the talking. 'My son is a professional footballer. He is lucky enough to be able to devote his life to his passion and is not unemployed as many people are today. Lots of the supporters who pay to come and watch him are working people, like me. The only thing they expect from him is that he plays well on the pitch. That's the only way he can show his attachment to Real and make sure that the fans stop whistling at him. The rest is irrelevant.' Antoine's father was tough. He said that he was not trying to make excuses for his son but that he hoped people would under-stand: 'He's been living away from the family home since he was fourteen. When Éric Olhats stopped being his confidant he began relying on Martín Lasarte. Now, from one day to the next, he's found himself alone.' But badly advised and influenced by his agent.

People in San Sebastián were not duped by the intentions of John Williams, whose contract with the player came to an end on 30 October 2011. It was said that he had pressur-ised Antoine over a transfer to Atlético Madrid so he could take a substantial cut with him when he left. Nor were any doubts cast on the young Antoine, a victim of his inexperience. 'They put him in front of a microphone, ask him if he liked Atlético, if he would like to play with Forlán, he says yes and they have their headline. That's how the scandal started,' explains Jorge Mendiola, a journalist with the *Diario Vasco*. 'In the same way, his comments at Clairefontaine provoked such an outcry that when he came back to the Zubieta, Antoine retreated into silence so he could concentrate on his football.'

Did that bring the matter to a close? It certainly looked that way. It seemed as if the boy had understood his mistake. Montanier accepted his apology and hoped he would now be able to focus properly on his football. They needed him to, given that Real were in the midst of the relegation battle. As the end of November approached, the club found itself next to bottom in the table and there were rumours of Montanier's imminent sacking. On 27 November, Real Sociedad were leading 2–0 against Real Betis at the Estadio Benito Villamarín but allowed themselves to be caught in incomprehensible fashion: the score was 2–2 and the Sevillan team had plenty of opportunities to take the lead. But in the 92nd minute, Iñigo Martínez fired what seemed like a laser-guided missile from the centre circle that found its way under the crossbar. Real Sociedad were ahead: 2–3. It was one of the goals of the season, as well as the lifeline needed by the French manager. The following week Real managed another victory at home to Malaga: a 3–2 win sealed in the 90th minute. It was followed by three draws, and, by the end of the year, Real had lifted themselves up the table. It was between late 2011 and early 2012 that Griezmann resurfaced. On 13 December, he distinguished himself with a fine match against Granada in the Copa del Rey, scoring the first goal in the 4–1 win and looking dangerous every time he had the ball at his feet. It was the first time in 23 years that Real had knocked a team from La Liga out of the Copa del Rey. It was also the first step in a reconciliation between Griezmann and the supporters. Things just got better and better and, on 14 January, against Valencia in Mestalla, Antoine scored again, his second league goal and his third of the season, securing all three points for his team.

'Everything was back to normal. After the controversy, the early difficulties due to a shortened preparation in the summer and problems with team performance, Antoine had once again become the darling of the fans,' remembers Philippe Montanier. 'Antoine showed he was mentally tough, that he could overcome a tricky time after the rumours about his transfer. He was no longer bothered by the story or the whistles from the supporters and he knew how to stay focused on his game. He showed me that he was a complete and technical player with great physical resistance, capable of putting in significant attacking and defensive work. He had great qualities and few weaknesses. Little by little, he progressed, gained strength and had a good season. He scored seven or eight goals and, despite his youth, was a key member of the squad, as you would expect a twenty year old to be.'

Montanier was not mistaken. Antoine ended the 2011–12 season with seven goals in 35 league matches and one goal in three Copa del Rey games. One more goal than the previous two years. Real, on 47 points, ended the season in twelfth place. No one was satisfied with this finish. A volley of criticism was aimed at Montanier, the man who it was hoped would bring about a radical change in the team's playing style following the departure of Lasarte. Nevertheless, at the end of the league season, the Frenchman, a former goalkeeper with Caen and Nantes, remained in the *txuri urdin* dugout as the following season loomed. Speculation about Antoine's future resurfaced during the summer transfer window. There was talk of Olympique Marseille because Jean-Pierre Bernès, his new agent, also represented Didier Deschamps, OM's manager at the time.

When the transfer window opened, a new contender was added to the list, Athletic Bilbao. But this time, Antoine did not let the journalists get one over on him when they asked if he was planning to leave Real. He replied with a frank and direct 'No!'

Chapter 17

The Little Devil

Matches played: 34
In the starting eleven: 32
Minutes played: 2,855
Goals: 10
Assists: 3
Yellow cards: 8
Red cards: 0

Antoine Griezmann's 2012–13 La Liga season in black and white. Stats fans will note that this does not include one Copa del Rey match in which he was in the starting eleven, played 77 minutes and scored a single goal. In total, Griezmann finished the season with eleven goals across all competitions, just behind the fourteen scored by Carlos Vela and the fifteen by Imanol Agirretxe, the team's two top scorers.

Let's look back at how the story unfolded from 12 July, as Antoine was posing for the new Real Sociedad Nike collection for the 2012–13 season. The event was held in the Gainditu building at the Zubieta in front of a roomful of sponsors, teammates, club employees and journalists. Xabi Prieto, the captain, modelled the blue and white striped shirt. Claudio Bravo, dressed from head to toe in green, unveiled the goalkeepers' strip. Imanol Agirretxe wore the away strip, an orange shirt and black shorts that had something of the Holland shirt worn by a certain Johan Cruyff about it. Antoine donned the electric blue training strip, which looked a lot like the France team colours. Griezmann, sporting a new haircut, was all smiles and promised plenty of innovation when it came to unusual goal celebrations. The new collection was tested for the first time in a friendly against Eglantins d'Hendaye on 14 July which resulted in a resounding 15–0 victory for the San Sebastián club. With the exception of the game against Eibar, their pre-season matches saw Real Sociedad go up against sparring partners from France (Lyon and Bordeaux) and Italy (Modena, Parma, Varese and Siena).

Real Sociedad appeared in their orange strip for the first time at 4pm on 20 July at the Stade Pavillon Bleu in Saint Jean de Luz. OL were their opposition. The game had added spice for Antoine, a former supporter of the Lyon club. It was a friendly, of course, but the number 7 was extremely motivated and gave his team the advantage in the 62nd minute. Sixteen minutes later, Mikel Gonzalez lost the ball resulting in a Lyonnais counter-attack finished by Jimmy Briand. The game ended in a 1–1 draw. Griezmann and Chori Castro, the Uruguayan originally from Trinidad who had arrived from Mallorca during the summer transfer window, were the best players on the pitch. The Basque press highlighted the French player's stunning form but Real Sociedad began its 67th season in La Liga in the worst possible way with a stinging 5–1 loss at home to Barcelona on 19 August. 'Like the previous year, the team struggled to be effective and seemed to still have the same problems,' said Montanier.

Eleven days later, Antoine's long-awaited contract extension was finally complete. On 30 August, at noon, the left-footed player signed a new agreement binding him to Real until 30 June 2016. Wearing a light-blue t-shirt and standing in the middle of the Anoeta pitch for the club channel

RSTV's camera, he announced: 'I'm very happy. I want my adventure here to continue. We've been talking about it for a year. Last month there was a lot of discussion with the president and we've finally reached an agreement. I'm happy to be staying at Real. I feel good here and I've always said that I didn't want to join another team. I still have plenty to learn. It's like a family here. A lot of people have put their trust in me and given me the chance to play in the first division. The president is building a great team and I want to be part of it.'

Real played Mallorca in Palma the following day. The French player wanted to bring three points home to San Sebastián and was keen to score because 'that would be the best way to celebrate my contract extension.' But things did not go as planned and the Basques lost 1–0. It was déjà-vu again: Real could win at home but kept losing on the road. On 30 September, between two disappointments at Levante and Betis, the Anoeta played host to a Basque derby that was more hotly anticipated than usual. Why? The interest from Marcelo Bielsa's Athletic Bilbao in Griezmann the previous June and the subsequent response from the president Aperribay, who had blown his top in an interview with *Teledonosti*: 'If they call about Griezmann we won't even pick up the phone!' he fumed. The jibes thrown in the direction of their rivals spiced up the derby and the young French player got involved, saying of his opponents: 'I don't follow them. I don't watch their matches.' These remarks drew anger from the Athletic fans and jeering rang out in the San Mamés. To make things worse, Real had lost its last three encounters with Bilbao, a negative trend that the *txuri urdin* supporters hoped to see reversed. Antoine heeded their wish, opening the scoring in the 62nd minute before Carlos Vela increased the lead from the penalty spot three minutes later. The game finished 2–0 and there was no doubt that the most pragmatic team had won. Vela, a Mexican from Cancún, had been at the club for a year. Initially on loan from Arsenal, he had joined Real Sociedad on a permanent basis in July for the €3 million needed to buy 50 per cent of his rights. Vela was the ideal partner for Griezmann. 'They had the same profile, the same way of playing, the same pace, the same vision of the game and thought highly of one another,' said Montanier. 'They had a great deal of under-standing and this was reflected on the pitch, where they were very effective. They worked really well that season.'

Unfortunately, as in the previous season, derby success was followed by two defeats at the Anoeta against Atlético Madrid and Espanyol. This did not go down well with the fans, who were once again calling for Montanier's head.

On 11 November, the club needed to bring three points home from an away game at Malaga to avoid dropping into the relegation zone. Suffering from a muscular injury, Antoine Griezmann did not take part. It was his second absence following the game against Espanyol. His teammates won 2–1 thanks to goals from Vela and Prieto and Real finally started to get off the ground with some very attractive foot-ball. But things did not go so well for Antoine. Apart from a consolation goal against Cordoba on 27 November 2012, which was not enough to prevent Real's exit from the Copa del Rey, the French player entered a goal drought that would last for several months.

Antoine Griezmann had become known as 'The Little Devil' in San Sebastián. The nickname had previously been given to Roberto López Ufarte (474 matches in La Liga and 128 goals for Real Sociedad, Atlético Madrid and Betis in the 1970s and 80s). It had all started at a tournament in Monte-Carlo in 1975 when the Spanish Under-18 side were playing in front of Prince Rainier III of Monaco. While watching the young offensive midfielder the prince asked '*Qui est ce petit diable?*' [Who is that little devil?]' The anecdote was reported by José Maria García, a Spanish journalist. The nickname given to Ufarte stuck and, with the emergence of Griezmann, comparisons between the two players multiplied. 'Whenever a small left-footed player came up from the Real academy, they would compare him to me and give him the same nickname,' Ufarte explained while sipping fruit juice in a bar in old San Sebastián. 'But I have to admit that Antoine, like every player who plays at the professional level nowadays, is better than those who played in my day. He strikes the ball better than I did, with more power, and is a better goalscorer than I was. But it's not only that: he knows how to organise the game, how to create space for his teammates and create opportunities. He's also very competitive. When he doesn't score, he just keeps on working until luck smiles on him again.'

On 10 February 2013, Griezmann once again found the back of the net at Real Zaragoza's Romareda stadium after a long wait. He opened the scoring and his team won 2–1. It was the turning point in his season and saw Real Sociedad begin their climb back up the table. He equalised at the San Mamés during the second derby of the season, won 3–1 by Real, scored twice in a 4–1 win over Valladolid and again in the 4–2 victory over Malaga. To top this off, he scored the only goal of the game against Deportivo de La Coruña at the Riazor on the final day of the Spanish league season. The goal saw Real clinch fourth place in the table and secure a Champions League spot. The Basque team finished ahead of Valencia by a single point after the Bats lost away at Sevilla. After a ten-year wait, the *txuri urdin* were back in Europe!

It was the icing on the cake at the end of a breath-taking season that deserved to be celebrated. Firstly, on the pitch, once the match was over, in front of the Basque fans who had made the trip. Then in the dressing room, where Asier Illaramendi and Iñigo Martínez kept their promise and shaved their heads. And finally, at the hotel, with speeches, appearances from the clubs' directors, singing and dancing. But the festivities did not end there since the majority of players were not going back to San Sebastián straight away. Several of them flew to Ibiza, where Dani Estrada, Real's right-winger, was holding his stag party. It goes without saying that Antoine was the hero of the night. He even managed to take a selfie with Mario Götze, the German midfielder who had just been transferred from Borussia Dortmund to Bayern Munich. 'Antoine is a lovely, generous and enthusiastic "little devil". He's constantly got a smile on his face and is always happy. He puts his teammates in a good mood because he's fun, spontaneous, always ready to laugh and joke. In the dressing room it was really entertaining to watch him dance and imitate rappers and singers who were popular at the time. But none of that took away from the fact that he was an exemplary player, a real hard-worker, serious at training and very popular with everyone,' explained Montanier.

Philippe Montanier left Real Sociedad on 4 June 2013 while the festivities were still in full swing in Ibiza. He had spent two magnificent seasons in San Sebastián and worked well with the club's young players, but the contract offered to him was not enough. 'It wasn't great,' he said. Instead he decided to accept a better offer from Stade Rennais and the two Frenchmen went their separate ways.

Chapter 18

Gerland, August 2013

Emotions like that are impossible to erase. 'Goooooooaaaaaaal!' He really had to pinch himself to believe it. 'It was amazing.' He could never have imagined it even in his wildest dreams. 'It was a wonderful bicycle kick.' Alain Griezmann has not forgotten anything about that warm summer evening. Even a year later, when a Spanish journalist arrived in Mâcon to talk about the rise of the child prodigy, the discussion rapidly turned to this famous match: the crucial first leg of the Champions League game between Olympique Lyonnais and Real Sociedad played on 20 August 2013 at the Stade de Gerland.

The Spanish journalist, Javier Villagarcía, had got things spot on. He brought Grizi's father a match scarf in the colours of both clubs. Alain Griezmann willingly accepted the gift, folding it carefully to show the Lyonnais side to the camera first: 'When Antoine was fourteen, he was a Lyon fan. I would take him to the match every Saturday.'

With a hint of irony, Antoine's father then showed the other side of the scarf with the Real Sociedad logo: 'If someone had told me back then that my son would play for Real Sociedad, I would have said they were mad!' But now they're Antoine's team,' he said, clasping the blue and white shield. 'It's the same for me. I don't watch the French league any more, now I watch La Liga. Every time Real Sociedad play I'm glued to my TV. We watch Lyon from time to time to see

Antoine's friend Alexandre Lacazette, but Sociedad is where his heart is. They're the ones who had faith in him and gave him his chance.'

Imagine the excitement when, on Friday 9 August 2013, at the stroke of noon, the draw for the preliminary round of the Champions League was made in Nyon (Switzerland). Six matches, including some shocks, came out of the hat: Fenerbahçe–Arsenal, Schalke 04–Metalist Kharkiv, Paços de Ferreira–Zenit Saint Petersburg, PSV Eindhoven–AC Milan and … Lyon–Real Sociedad.

It was the perfect draw: 'The opponents I wanted,' Antoine said at the press conference that followed. For him the match-up was perfect for a number of reasons: it was the opportunity to chase away his old demons once and for all against what had once been his favourite club – which had rejected him at the age of thirteen – and to finally tread the pitch at the Stade de Gerland, something he had dreamed about so often as a kid. It was also an opportunity to impress the French public and national team directors.

On the afternoon of 9 August, the phone lines between Lyon and San Sebastián were ringing hot. There were messages of encouragement from family and friends who had already booked their evening out at the Stade de Gerland to support him in the first leg. There were also texts and calls to the Lyonnais players in the France team: Alexandre Lacazette, Clément Grenier and Gueïda Fofana, with whom Antoine had won the Under-19 Euros in 2010 and reached the semi-final of the Under-20 World Cup in 2011. In both camps the news was treated with some gentle banter in advance of the key two-leg tie.

For the Basque team, this qualifying round was undoubtedly the first highlight of the 2013–14 season. An unmissable night despite the troubling off-season: Philippe Montanier had been replaced by Jagoba Arrasate, who, at 35 years of age, had experienced a meteoric rise. Just three years after his return to the club as director of the youth teams in the role of assistant to Montanier during the 2012–13 season, this modest ex-player saw himself propelled to the head of the team that had finished fourth in the previous Liga season. This was not particularly reassuring, especially given that the club had also allowed its centrepiece midfielder, Asier Illarramendi, to leave for Real Madrid for €32 million. Esteban Granero had arrived on loan from QPR to replace him. Up front, the young Swiss player, Haris Seferović (Fiorentina) arrived to complete the strike force alongside the trio of Agirretxe, Vela and Griezmann.

This recruitment was fairly meagre in the face of Champions League pressure, especially as Antoine did not seem to be in the best physical shape when it came to making a start on preparations: 'He came back from holiday over-weight and carrying some muscular issues,' said Arrasate, now the manager of CD Numancia. 'I was a bit worried because there wasn't much time before the vital early season matches and our focus was fully on the Champions League. But Antoine was reassuring, he told me there was no need to worry, that he would work hard over the coming weeks to be ready for the big day, the Champions League qualifying round. I had faith in him.'

Antoine was used sparingly during the preparatory matches. On 17 August 2013, he was substituted in the first Liga match, a 2–0 win over Getafe at the Anoeta. Even on the bench, debate still raged around him just a few days before the trip to Lyon for the first leg. His early exile had provided plenty of newspaper fodder since the draw. There was also an incredible quirk of fate: on 10 March 2004, he had been in the stands at the Stade de Gerland for Real Sociedad's last European game. The Basque team were beaten 1–0 and sent packing by Olympique Lyonnais in the return leg of the Champions League knock-out round. That night, after the winning Lyonnais goal scored by Juninho, Antoine told his father that he 'wanted to play in those kind of matches one day.'

Nine years later his dream had come true. He was preparing to make his European debut at the Gerland, but in a Sociedad shirt. 'I'm really happy to be here,' he said on the eve of the match when he appeared at a press conference alongside his manager Arrasate and captain Xabi Prieto. 'Coming back to this stadium is very emotional. It was here that I watched some great Champions League matches wearing a Sonny Anderson shirt. I was here for the match against Sociedad and plenty of others, including a Lyon-Barça game when Juninho scored a superb free kick almost from the corner post. I'm not here with any feelings of revenge. I'm just very happy to be playing a game in France.'

20 August 2013, 8.40pm. Olympique Lyonnais and Real Sociedad take to the pitch in front of 40,000 spectators in the Gerland. The stadium is full and the Basque supporters have come in large numbers. They occupy part of the south curve as well as a section of the Jean Bouin stand parallel to the pitch. The French club is wearing its classic white strip. The Real Sociedad players have abandoned their blue and white shirts for a black outfit devoid of any sponsorship. Antoine is the last to climb the stairs to face the public. As if he wants to savour it a little longer. His hair is dyed completely blond, as it was when he had his trial aged thirteen.

The images of his failures and the battles he has since won must be running through his mind when the official anthem of the Champions League begins to ring out.

The two teams line up. Antoine glances at the Jean-Jaures

stand, where his friends and family are. He is trying to find his father, who must be filled with emotion to finally see him play on the turf at the Stade de Gerland.

The music comes to an end. Protocol allows the number 7 to greet some familiar faces, including his friends Gueïda Fofana, Clément Grenier and Alex Lacazette, with whom he shares an uncomplicated hug. The match can begin. Antoine is in the starting eleven on the left in a three-pronged attack with Carlos Vela on the right and Seferović as centre forward. Arrasate has finally placed his trust in him. An all or nothing bet for the new Sociedad coach. He would not regret it.

The whistle blows. The Serbian referee starts the game. The Griezmann show can begin.

In the fifth minute, Liassine Cadamuro, another player neglected by French football only to be discovered by Éric Olhats and Real Sociedad in 2008, picks out Antoine with a long pass down the left wing. It is almost his first touch. He controls it just beyond the midfield, then embarks on a lengthy run along the touchline to flummox his man-marker, Miguel Lopes. The Portuguese international makes a clumsy tackle, allowing Antoine to get around him, lift his head and find Carlos Vela in space. The Mexican's strike just misses the goal. The French team have been given a warning. It is the first clue as to Grizou's form.

'You could see Griezmann's talent in this very first move,' according to the French TV pundit Christian Bassila. 'This duel between the Real Sociedad number 7 and Miguel Lopes promised to be one of the keys to the match.'

In the sixteenth minute, Real Sociedad intensify their dominance. Vela, who had hit the post four minutes earlier, is at the heart of a move that sees the commentator get carried away:

'Vela is in an offside position but hasn't been spotted.

He tries to find Griezmann who goes in with a bicycle kick – and opens the scoring with a magnificent strike by Real Sociedad's French player. What a goal! As a child he dreamt of playing in the Champions League for OL and now he's scored the first goal of tonight's game with an unforgettable move. The boy from Mâcon has helped Real Sociedad strike an important blow.'

It took just a few seconds. On the screens in the press gallery, journalists were marvelling at the wonder goal, calling it magical and fantastic. On the bench, Arrasate had no need for the onslaught of slow motion replays to savour the talent of his striker: 'I remember the cross from Vela, which didn't look all that threatening, but Antoine managed to turn it into something exceptional. He jumped with such beauty, harmony and athleticism to strike the ball with his left foot and find the back of the net. He had done similar things in training but never in a match! It was one of the best goals he had ever scored. It was also very important for our qualification.'

The Lyonnais players were merely spectators. The Cameroonian defender, Henri Bedimo had been wrong-footed and could do nothing but watch and admire the move. The feet of the goalkeeper, Anthony Lopes, had turned to stone and he was powerless as the ball hit the bottom left hand corner of his netting.

It was a sensational return to his home country. All the more so because Antoine did not stop there. During the minutes that followed, he continued to run rings around the Lyonnais defenders, making the club even sorrier they had not done everything they could to reel him in some years earlier.

In the 23rd minute, Antoine found himself on the end of a long clearance from his keeper Claudio Bravo and in a tussle with Gueïda Fofana. He managed to hold off his former France youth team teammate before unleashing a tight-angled left-footed shot that Anthony Lopes somehow managed to keep out.

'What was amazing', continues Arrasate, 'is that there was a huge amount of expectation on him before that match. But he knew how to use that pressure and turn it into something positive. His goal, as well as his overall performance, helped him be seen in a new light in France, because his potential was already well known in Spain.'

In the second half, the Basques scored a second goal in the 50th minute with a stunning strike from Seferović. Antoine played his part with the penultimate pass. In the 70th minute, Antoine was replaced by Chori Castro. His return to France had not disappointed. Despite grabbing a goal and an assist, he left the Gerland with a grimace on his face and a left shoulder injury as the French fans whistled his departure.

He was all anyone could talk about in the post-match discussions. Even on the OLTV channel, as the Spanish *Euronews* journalist, Juan-Antonio Aldeondo, painted a eulogistic portrait: 'His performance is not surprising. He has reached a psychological milestone and matured this season. Luckily he doesn't score goals like that every weekend, if he did he would have left Real Sociedad already.'

With a question mark hanging over him for much of the lead-up to the return leg thanks to his shoulder injury, Antoine would confirm his promise on the pitch at the Anoeta on 28 August 2013.

In the 55th minute, he provided Carlos Vela with an assist from a corner for another 2–0 win over Olympique Lyonnais.

Grizou did not miss the chance to find his feet on the European stage. An exceptional goal and an assist to send

Real Sociedad into the Champions League group phase. The follow-up to this apprenticeship would be more painful. Five defeats and a single but prestigious 0–0 draw at home to Manchester United, and, as a result, a last place finish in Group A behind the Red Devils, Bayer Leverkusen and Shakhtar Donetsk. Like his team, Antoine had nothing to celebrate, with no goals or assists in six starts. He had tasted football at the highest level and enjoyed two important duels with the English side. He had had the opportunity to visit Old Trafford and the wonderful atmosphere of the Theatre of Dreams. He had been able to see what still separated him from top players of the calibre of Ryan Giggs and Wayne Rooney. Like all future greats, he would soon learn from these knocks.

Chapter 19

Boom

It was just six days before Christmas. At the Zubieta, Real were preparing for their final match of 2013. The players and technical staff were arriving at the training centre in dribs and drabs. They parked their cars and filed straight into the dressing rooms to change and get ready for the debrief session following the match against Algeciras. The programme included a warm-down session for those who had played in the Copa del Rey the day before and a technical and tactical session for the others in advance of the trip to the Nuevo Los Carmenes stadium, where Real would face Granada. The routine was the same as every other working day. But this 19 December was a little different. Father Christmas was on his way. With his long white beard, bright red suit and cap, he sneaked into the dressing room, silently and secretly, with a bag full of presents. There was one for every member of the first team, not forgetting the stewards and coaches. Yes, Antoine Griezmann had decided to dress up as the man children all over the world await impatiently on Christmas Eve. Without telling anyone, he went shopping at the FNAC media store before coming to the Zubieta in the appropriate outfit to surprise everyone. He distributed the presents before inevitably immortalising the moment with a photograph posted to Twitter and other social networks.

This was Antoine's way of thanking those who had helped him achieve his best ever season. He had already scored ten league goals, equalling his record for the entire 2012–13 season. He may not have scored since the seventh match of the season (Real Sociedad–Sevilla, 1–1) but that was not the full story: there was also his magnificent return to Lyon in the Champions League, which had got people talking about him across Europe, and two performances in the Copa del Rey. One of his cup appearances had come just the day before, on 18 December, with a 4–0 win over Algeciras at the Anoeta, sending the Basque club into the last sixteen of the competition. Thirteen goals did not guarantee happiness but they contributed to the joy and carefree attitude of Griezmann. How could he explain the incredible period he was experiencing? He simply put it down to more experience and that this had helped him enormously on the pitch. He tried to give the best of himself in every match and, towards the end of 2013, this finally paid off. On the other hand, what disappointed and irritated him was that he had failed to find the net in the group phase of the Champions League. He had had chances, against Bayer Leverkusen in particular, but to no avail. 'I'm not letting it go to my head,' confessed Antoine in a press conference. 'I'm satisfied because I've tried to help my team as much as possible. And I think the fans have noticed and appreciated that. They proved it when they gave me an ovation during the last match. It's important now to take the lessons from this to get back to the Champions League next season. It was a fantastic experience to play in that competition with the club that trained me.'

His thirteen goals had done Real Sociedad a power of good. After the 5–1 victory against Betis at home on 15 December, their third successive win in the Liga, the *txuri urdin* had picked up 26 points and found themselves sixth in the table, not far off fourth, which would see them qualify for the preliminary round of the Champions League for the second year in a row. Early elimination from the Champions League and the 'Griezmann dependency' were not such a bad thing in themselves.

Thirteen goals made Antoine the player of the moment; he was in fashion and top European clubs were keen to attract him to their ranks. Juventus, PSG, Arsenal and Chelsea were the calibre of names being bandied about. There were even rumours of the young man's possible departure during the winter transfer window. But this was nipped in the bud by both Jagoba Arrasate and Griezmann. 'He is happy, fully focused on his work and wants to continue growing. One thing is certain, we can take advantage of him here alongside us until June and, personally, I hope he'll continue his adventure here after that,' said the manager.

'I don't think I'm going to leave in January,' said Antoine, reassuringly. 'I'm not worried by rumours; my one and only aim at the moment is to do well here.'

Thirteen goals also gave France plenty to dream about because, Real's number 7 was the best French goalscorer in Europe in 2013, ahead of players such as Olivier Giroud and Karim Benzema. All this raised the temperature on the other side of the Pyrenees and Real's press officer was struggling to handle all the interview requests coming from France.

Thirteen goals and he had no intention of stopping there. Against Granada, on 22 December, the pearl of the *txuri urdin* scored the second goal in the 3–1 win over the Andalusians. Griezmann began 2014 as he had finished the previous year, opening the score in the Basque derby, won 2–0 on 5 January.

'He had an exceptional first half of the season, scoring a huge number of goals, including twelve in the league if my memory serves me correctly. He's shown, as he has at Real in the past, his ability to improve and surpass himself year after year. He said he wanted to become one of the best players in the world. In that sense he was very professional because he would keep training, even after the sessions were over, practising corners, free kicks and penalties without stopping. He was a perfectionist: if things weren't going the way he wanted, he would start again and again until he had it just right. He did all that despite the fact that he also liked to joke around, act the clown, pull pranks, sing and laugh. On the pitch, he usually played on the left wing for us,' explained Arrasate, 'although he liked to come back into the middle and go up into the box. He was free to switch with Carlos Vela. He was extremely versatile and had the gift of being in the right place at the right time. He would appear out of nowhere, when no one was expecting him. That always surprised defenders. He was a kid with plenty of maturity and he deserved everything he earned.'

This maturity was also owed to his girlfriend, Erika. 'She helped him focus on football, on his career and on having the lifestyle of a professional player,' explained Miguel González, a journalist for the *Diario Vasco.* 'She's made me better, both at home and on the pitch,' confessed Antoine.

Erika Choperena, who turned 25 on 2017, originally from Vera de Bidasoa in Navarre, is a teaching graduate with a passion for fashion and her own trends and styling blog 'Cordialmente Erika'; she is from a good family, elegant, quiet and extremely discreet. She met Antoine in San Sebastián in 2011 and it took almost a year for him to win her over. They eventually started dating and it was not long before she appeared in the stands at the Anoeta to support her boyfriend. They then decided to move in together and the daily life of Real's number 7 gradually began to change. The boy now preferred staying at home with Erika, going to the beach, out for dinner or to the Donostia Arena to watch

Griezmann celebrates scoring against Real Madrid at the Anoeta Stadium, 18 September 2010
Juan Herrero/Epa/REX/Shutterstock

A delighted Griezmann wheels away after giving Real Sociedad the lead against Olympique Lyon at Stade de Gerland, 20 August 2013
Yoan Valat/Epa/REX/Shutterstock

(above) Arriving at the press conference to announce his move
to Atlético Madrid, 28 July 2014
Juan Herrero/Epa/REX/Shutterstock

(below) Griezmann goes up against Jonas Hector (L) and Mats Hummels of Germany
at Stade de France on the night of the Paris terror attacks, 13 November 2015
Jeffroy Guy/SIPA/REX/Shutterstock

Celebrating giving France the lead against the Republic of Ireland at Euro 2016, 26 June 2016
Yuri Kochetkov/Epa/ REX/Shutterstock

(*below*) A dejected Griezmann watches on as Portugal celebrate Eder's extra time winner in the Euro 2016 Final, 10 July 2016
Srdjan Suki/Epa/ REX/Shutterstock

(*above*) Receiving
the Euro 2016
'Player of the
Tournament' trophy,
7 October 2016
Ian Langsdon/Epa/REX/
Shutterstock

Kissing the World
Cup trophy after
beating Croatia in
the final in Moscow,
15 July 2018
Matthias Schrader/AP/
Shutterstock

Gipuzkoa Basketball Club matches with her and his friends. The results on the pitch were immediate. Or rather, had been. During the second half of the season, Antoine lost his sparkle. His last strokes of brilliance dated back to between late January and late February. On 26 January 2014, against Elche at the Anoeta, the number 7 was at it again. In the second minute, on the end of a deep ball from Carlos Vela, he made for the goal and threw a shot up over the head of Toño, the opposing keeper. Then, in the eleventh minute, a cross from Xabi Prieto found its target as Antoine jumped to connect with the ball at an angle that was impossible for the keeper to reach. Griezmann had scored twice in nine minutes. After Vela's goal to make it 3–0, he got his hat trick, the only one he would score for Real. Griezmann pounced on a fumbled cross to volley the ball into the back of the net, sealing a 4–0 win. It was the 73rd minute and Antoine celebrated his goal with a slide across the sodden turf of the Anoeta. It was his fifteenth goal in the Liga, making him one of the leading lights of the Spanish league, only outshone by Cristiano Ronaldo and Diego Costa. It was a shame that the first goal, a subtle lob that had come so early in the match, was eventually attributed to Damián Suárez, who, in a desperate attempt to clear the ball, had eventually pushed it into the back of his own net. In the end that was what the statistics would say. One goal fewer, making it 'only' fourteen goals for the French player, to which another was added during the 3–1 win inflicted, to general surprise, by Real Sociedad on Barça at home. It was a response, or rather revenge for the Copa del Rey elimination eleven days earlier. On 12 February, during the return semi-final against the *Blaugrana*, Antoine managed to equalise after an early goal from Messi. The final score was 1–1 but Barça's 2–0 victory in the first leg, at Camp Nou, sent the Catalans into the final.

After the goal against Barça in the league, the lights went off and the curtain came down. The prolific rhythm of the player with the golden left foot seemed to have stopped dead. Between 23 February and 17 May, the end of the Liga season, Antoine Griezmann scored just once, on 12 April in a 2–2 draw against Celta Vigo. That took his total to sixteen league goals and twenty across all competitions, in addition to three assists. That was it; the goal machine had shuddered to a halt. Mauri Idiakez, a sharp-tongued journalist with *Cadena Cope*, provided his own explanation: 'Over the last three months, he couldn't have cared less. He wanted to play for France in the World Cup and didn't want to get injured. He was just thinking about Brazil and where he would play next season. Because one thing was certain, he wanted to take the leap he hadn't been allowed to take in the summer of 2011.' Real, thanks to Antoine's goal drought and the lack of motivation of his teammates, had plunged from fifth to seventh in the end of season table, a position that would not see them qualify to play in their beloved Champions League. It was Atlético Madrid who won the league, on the final day, thanks to a victory at Camp Nou. A week later they would play in the Champions League final against Real Madrid in Lisbon. The *Colchoneros* showed plenty of promise.

Chapter 20

Back in Blue

Celebrated with a selfie. In the foreground of the picture, with his smartphone in his right hand, the Olympique Lyonnais midfielder Clément Grenier is all smiles. Taken in the back of a luxury car that looks a bit like a London taxi, he is trying to sneak into the shot in front of those sitting on either side. His travelling companions are not just anyone but no fewer than four French internationals: the AS Saint-Étienne defender, Loïc Perrin, two other OL players, midfielder Maxime Gonalons and striker Alexandre Lacazette, and, right up against the left rear door behind the driver, the 'Spaniard' Antoine Griezmann. They are all beaming from ear to ear.

On 21 May 2014, these five French footballers are on the threshold of history. They are setting off on a mission, as demonstrated by the caption that accompanies the photo on Clément Grenier's Twitter account: 'Taxi to Clairefontaine.' Grenier adds two emojis of a football and the French flag to these few words. He also includes the hashtag #TeamFrance.

The small group from the Rhône-Alpes is en route to Clairefontaine, the national centre for French football, where Les Bleus are about to begin their preparation for the 2014 World Cup, due to take place in Brazil from 12 June to 14 July. Knowing this makes it easier to understand the excitement emanating from the picture.

Eight days earlier, on 13 May, the manager, Didier

Deschamps, put an end to the unbearable suspense and delivered a list of 30 names on the TF1 stage live on the eight o'clock news: seven reserves, including Gonalons, Perrin and Lacazette – smiling the least in the photos – and 23 other squad members heading to the home of football. These lucky ones included Antoine Griezmann!

Antoine was seven years old when he discovered the happiness that watching matches on TV, sprawled with his family on the sofa, could bring. Wearing his white shorts and blue shirt that was too big for him, printed with Zidane's number 10, he had his first experience of success as a fan. Alongside Théo and Maud, he draped himself in the Tricolore to celebrate each and every goal on the balcony of the house in Les Gautriats. He even went with his friend Jean-Baptiste Michaud to welcome his idols at the Mâcon-Loché TGV station when the France team arrived to train at Saint-Jean d'Ardières before their match against Denmark in Lyon. The *M6* cameras fleetingly spotted two small blond heads crowding around the players in search of autographs. That was 1998 and sixteen years later Antoine was about to take up the baton.

His selection was formalised by Didier Deschamps on 27 February 2014. The French coach revealed the squad of 23 players selected for a friendly against the Netherlands to the press. Antoine had got into this final World Cup warm-up match by the skin of his teeth. He was one of seven strikers selected for the sold out game at the Stade de France in Saint-Denis. Alongside him up front would be Karim Benzema (Real Madrid), one of his idols whose shirt he had bought when he was the jewel in the crown at Olympique Lyonnais. There was also Olivier Giroud (Arsenal), Dimitri Payet (Marseille), Loïc Rémy (Newcastle), Franck Ribéry (Bayern Munich) and Mathieu Valbuena (Marseille).

How did Antoine learn the news? Just like the general public, he was sitting on his sofa, in front of his TV, with his girlfriend, Erika. It was a big moment. Joy, excitement and immediate pressure. His first reaction came through the official *txuri urdin* website: 'I've worked hard and that's why I'm happy to be part of this team. The World Cup is my aim now, it's a dream for any player.' He also marked it on his Twitter account: 'Happy to be part of the squad! This is just the beginning. Keep working! #proud #happy #TeamFrance #dream.'

On 5 March 2014, Antoine was in the starting eleven for his first game for the senior team, a friendly against the Netherlands. His entire family were in the stands at the Stade de France to savour this magical moment. It was the start of a great love story with Les Bleus. It began with a magisterial *Marseillaise* (the French national anthem). 'The manager had always told me to play freely. But when you hear your first *Marseillaise* it's not that easy to control your emotions. I almost cried during the anthem,' the new international would recognise some time later. 'I saw my parents opposite me and I had to look up to the sky to make sure I didn't start crying. I was in the starting eleven so I had to deal with it.' It was not easy to keep a handle on his emotions. He was obviously weighed down against the Dutch. He struggled to free himself and to channel his desire to play, his willingness to show what he was capable of.

Antoine played 68 minutes before being replaced by Loïc Rémy. It was not enough to score – the two goals that gave France the win came from Benzema and Matuidi – but enough to show some promise on the left wing and a natural understanding with Benzema. Post-match opinions were divided: 'He showed willing but didn't seem all that comfortable,' said some. 'Will we see him for Les Bleus again?' 'Positive overall,' said others, answering the question already.

Yes, Antoine would be taking a summer trip to Brazil. After finding his quarters at Clairefontaine with his friends Lacazette and Grenier, he could take advantage of three World Cup warm-up games and the back pain that kept Franck Ribéry away from the team day after day, gradually cementing his place on the left wing. On 27 May at the Stade de France, he started for a second time against Norway, a 4–0 win, failed to score and came off after an hour but was named the best French player of the first half. Five days later, in Nice, he replaced Rémy half an hour from the end of the game against Paraguay. The score was still 0–0. After several fumbled balls, he did not miss his first real chance in the 81st minute: the ball fell to him after an Olivier Giroud header. He was on the left, at least a good two metres from the penalty area. He had the time to control the ball despite the threatening defenders and struck with his right foot. The ball flew over the head of three Paraguayans and into Silva's net. Goal! The Mâconnais' first for the senior team.

The equaliser for Paraguay by Caceres (1–1) at the end of the match would do nothing to take away from the happiness of Antoine, who was granted two days rest by Deschamps to enjoy his first goal for France with his family in Mâcon. A week later, he again scored points in the final warm-up match played this time in Lille against Jamaica. On 8 June, French morale was high after a flood of goals. 8–0. Goals from Cabaye and Giroud, with braces from Matuidi, Benzema and Griezmann. In just twenty minutes on the pitch, the Real striker found a way to show what he could do on two occasions: once on the end of a cross from Benzema, missed by Valbuena, which Antoine converted with a right-footed shot that grazed the post (77th minute), then a pass from the left from Moussa Sissoko that Antoine lined up at the near post to fool the keeper with a sublime backheel. The number 11 celebrated his two goals with Sissoko. Three goals in three warm-up games; Griezmann was ready for his first World Cup. Brazil here we come!

FRANCE 3–0 HONDURAS
15 June 2014, Estádio Beira-Rio (Porto Alegre)

Deschamps's Bleus got their 2014 World Cup off to a great start. 3–0. The perfect score in their first game. Benzema took charge and scored two goals that looked like three: 1–0 from the penalty spot (43rd minute); 2–0 after an own goal by the keeper Valladares following a strike from the Madrid player that came back off the post (48th minute); 3–0 – the finest – a powerful shot from the right of the box, from a close angle under the crossbar (72nd minute). A job well done. Antoine played the whole match and enjoyed his first appearance in the greatest of competitions. He also narrowly missed scoring his first goal in the 23rd minute. On the end of a cross from Evra, he jumped higher than the Honduran defender, Figueroa and got his head onto it but the ball struck the crossbar. He was out of luck but his performance on the left wing and his widely praised understanding with Benzema and Valbuena had led to the biggest French absentee from the competition, Franck Ribéry, being forgotten.

SWITZERLAND 2–5 FRANCE
20 June 2014, Arena Fonte Nova (Salvador de Bahia)

A treat if you get to play. Frustrating from the bench if you don't. For the second Group E match, Antoine was a substitute. The game had already been heralded as the group's decider. The winner would be better placed in the round of sixteen by sealing top of the group. Deschamps had decided to give Olivier Giroud a start and moved Benzema to the left at Griezmann's expense. Unlike Antoine against Honduras, the Arsenal striker did not let his first opportunity pass him by: in the seventeenth minute, his diagonal header was accurate and ended up in the top corner. 1–0. Matuidi, Valbuena, Benzema and Sissoko took turns at scoring. What a demonstration! 5–0 for France in the 73rd minute. On the touchline, Antoine intensified his warm-up. Just as he was coming on for Valbuena, the Swiss scored through Dzemali. Xhaka would eventually pull the score back to 5–2, while Benzema was unfairly deprived of a fourth goal in this World Cup in injury time. Antoine had almost nothing to get his teeth into.

ECUADOR 0–0 FRANCE
5 June 2014, Maracanã Stadium (Rio de Janeiro)

The Maracanã, a childhood dream. A crowd of 73,000 attended Ecuador versus France and Griezmann's second start in the World Cup. He was still on the left wing for the French attack but this time it was nothing like the demonstration against the Swiss. The match was tight and ragged but Antoine came close to providing an assist to Pogba from a free kick just before half time. At the resumption, he was still the most dangerous French striker. In the 47th minute, Antoine perfectly followed up a move that began with a burst of pace from Sagna down the right wing. His pick-up was deflected by Domínguez onto the cross bar. For the second time in the tournament, Grizi had struck the woodwork. The final score was 0–0. Replaced in the 79th minute, the Sociedad stalwart was one of the few French players not to have disappointed. France qualified all the same and topped Group E ahead of Switzerland.

FRANCE 2–0 NIGERIA
30 June 2014, Estádio Nacional (Brasilia)

Les Bleus prepared meticulously for this decisive match at their base in Ribeirão Preto, where they had been staying since their arrival in Brazil. Once again Deschamps decided to alternate things up front. As had been the case against Switzerland, Giroud was in the starting eleven. Deschamps was banking on his physique and aerial presence to tire out the Nigerian defence. Benzema and Valbuena would take care of the wings. Griezmann was back on the bench.

The first hour of play was dire. Nigeria posed Les Bleus a huge number of problems. On two occasions, the French came close to disaster: in the nineteenth minute, Emmanuel Emenike was denied the opportunity to open the scoring by a marginal offside ruling. In the 39th minute, Peter Odemwingie saw his appeals following a clear foul by Patrice Evra fall on deaf ears. France offered nothing in attack apart from one opportunity for Paul Pogba. The relationship between Benzema, Giroud and Valbuena was non-existent. Deschamps had to react quickly. In the 62nd minute, he made his first change, replacing Olivier Giroud with Antoine Griezmann. Miraculously, the score was still 0–0. As if by magic, in the minutes that followed, the French finally began to play. The repositioning of Benzema as a number 9 and his clear understanding with Griezmann allowed the French to be more dangerous. Benzema took advantage of a one-two with Antoine to do what he needed with the ball, sliding it under Enyeama before it was cleared off the line by Victor Moses.

In the 79th minute, Paul Pogba finally unlocked the situation from a Valbuena corner (1–0). Les Bleus finished strongly, and, after injury time, Valbuena put in a low cross from a corner played back to Benzema. Griezmann was lying in wait in front of Enyeama but was beaten to it by Yobo, who scored an own goal. 2–0. Antoine had changed the course of the match. France reached the quarter-final of the World Cup and their number 11 had certainly caught the eye. His partners in attack were big fans:

Mathieu Valbuena: 'He's someone who can bring a lot of speed to the game thanks to his touch on the ball and his pace. It's a very good thing for us.'

Karim Benzema: 'Antoine worked hard on the wing, he gave us more depth than we had in the first half.'

FRANCE 0–1 GERMANY
30 June 2014, Maracanã Stadium (Rio de Janeiro)

'Lloris in goal; Sakho, Varane, Debuchy and Evra in defence; Pogba, Cabaye and Matuidi in midfield; Valbuena, Benzema and Griezmann in a three-pronged attack.' The French team almost picked itself. The team that had shone against Switzerland was back. Only Giroud was out of the starting eleven in favour of Griezmann, whose presence had changed the game against Nigeria.

Deschamps was hoping this would be the team to get the better of Joachim Löw's Germany. Like Les Bleus, *Die Mannschaft* had been blowing hot and cold since the start of the competition: they had swept aside Ronaldo's Portugal 4–0 in their first group match, but also conceded twice in a 2–2 draw against Ghana, and eventually made it through by the back door in the last sixteen against Algeria, winning 2–1 after extra time.

5pm, local time. *La Marseillaise* rang out first around the Maracanã. It was followed by the German anthem, *Das Lied der Deutschen*, which was sung loudly by the goalkeeper Manuel Neuer, the captain Philipp Lahm and the two giants Müller and Klose.

Just a few yards away, Antoine seemed impassive. It was just a front; he was, of course, boiling over inside: 'You're representing your country! There's nothing better than that. You could play for the best club in the world but it's worth nothing compared to playing for your national team.'

The whistle was blown by the Argentinian referee, Nestor Pitana. The first quarter-final of the World Cup 2014 had begun.

In the eighth minute, Benzema's first strike went wide; in the thirteenth minute, Toni Kroos measured a free kick perfectly for Mats Hummels. At 6ft 3in, the Borussia Dortmund defender got the better of Varane to fire a powerful header under the bar. Goal! Germany 1, France 0.

France already had their backs against the wall. They had to react. Antoine was struggling up front, running all over the place and calling for the ball. In the eighteenth minute Pogba looked for him but Boateng intervened; in the 24th minute, a deep ball from Cabaye was not accurate enough; in the 27th minute, he called for the ball on the left wing but it was again too deep; in the 32nd minute, Matuidi's pass was good but Neuer was one step ahead; in the 34th minute, he managed to escape the German defenders for once and crossed for Valbuena, who controlled the ball, and unleashed a shot but it was turned around the post by Neuer. Half time.

In the dressing room Les Bleus were encouraged by the fifteen minute break. They told themselves there was still all to play for. It was true that the Germans had proved nothing during the first half. Antoine was more energised than ever.

In the 46th minute, Benzema turned supplier but Grizi's touch deserted him and he lost his balance just as he was about to strike. In the 53rd minute came another chance but Antoine lost control once again just as he was about to challenge Neuer. His finishing left a lot to be desired. It was a shame because every time he put on a burst of pace the Germans struggled: first Khedira then Schweinsteiger were warned in turn after being ridiculed by the young French striker.

But it was not enough and the final minutes of the game arrived. Legs were heavy and thighs began to burn. There was no question of giving up. Lloris had pulled off a small miracle from a close range shot by Schürrle, a save that would keep Les Bleus in the match. Deschamps had to throw everything he had onto the pitch. Loïc Rémy and Olivier Giroud were late replacements for Benzema and Griezmann.

Injury time arrived. It was clear that the Germans were not comfortable. An opportunity would present itself, that was certain, and it came in the 94th minute:

Benzema picked up the ball on the left wing. The angle was tight but his strike was good. France were going to equalise, but no! Neuer once again pulled off a miraculous save to keep the ball out with his forearm.

It was over. Les Bleus had gone out of the World Cup. They ended up on their knees or lying on the turf at the Maracanã. Some got up quickly. Antoine's face was buried in his blue shirt. He was crying. Varane, Cissoko, Mavuba, Rémy and even the captain, Hugo Lloris took turns in comforting him, but he was inconsolable. At that moment, he was overwhelmed by his emotions. He was angry and distressed because France had more than enough to make it to the final stages of the competition. 'We could have eaten them for breakfast,' said Antoine a little later, once he had dried his tears. 'A World Cup in Brazil only happens once in your lifetime but it was a great honour to have been with Les Bleus and an important learning experience for the future.'

Chapter 21

Goodbye Real, Hello Atlético

'I've spent ten incredible years here. I arrived a child and am leaving a man. You were the first and only ones to believe in me. It wasn't easy for me at Real to start with. After several years at the training academy, where I worked hard and sacrificed a lot, I made it to the first team with the sole aim of playing at the highest level. Once again, thanks to your unconditional support, I succeeded.

'Now, all I can do is thank you for everything, for helping me to mature and for teaching me everything I know. And for allowing me to make my dream come true: to live out my passion, football. I would like to thank everyone by name but that would be impossible. I would at least like to say thank you to the coaches I have spent time with, for having faith in me and asking more from me when the time was right. Thank you to the directors for their support, in the good as well as in the bad times. Thank you to the technical and medical staff, without whom nothing would have been the same. Thank you to the journalists for your comments and for the experience you have given me. Thank you to my teammates and former teammates for making me believe in what I was doing both on and off the pitch. And of course thank you to you, the fans, for your unconditional support, day after day.

'After making my dreams come true, playing in the first division and the Champions League with the club that trained me, I needed to set myself new goals and new challenges. This summer, Atlético offered me this opportunity. An opportunity I could not refuse and I will do my best to honour it. Believe me, even if I am no longer wearing a Real Sociedad shirt and not living in San Sebastián, I will never forget the time I have spent here.'

It was a farewell letter addressed to Real Sociedad. Also a farewell to his childhood and his adolescence. The letter turned an important page in his life in order to open another, that of his adulthood and hopes for the future. Leaving Real Sociedad was to dare, to jump: from the provinces to the capital, from a cocoon to wider horizons. A leap forward in order to grow a little more.

The letter was read on 28 July 2014. It was 7pm at the Zubieta when Antoine began speaking, reciting it from memory, almost word for word, during an impromptu press conference. He had come to say goodbye to his former teammates. They had just finished training ahead of a Europa League tie against Aberdeen. Antoine had come back from Madrid, where he had passed the customary medical. He had come to collect his things and to ask the club for permission to talk to the media. It was just a few minutes, without even a single question, just these nervously-spoken words. Then, Griezmann, wearing a short-sleeved grey t-shirt and sporting a moustache and goatee beard, left.

A few hours earlier, around 11am, the announcement had been made official: 'Real Sociedad and Atlético Madrid have reached an agreement in principle concerning the transfer of Antoine Griezmann to the Madrid team,' explained the press release from the Basque club. 'Real Sociedad would like to thank Antoine for his professionalism and the dedication he has shown during his years at the club. The management wishes him all the best for the future, both personally and professionally.'

After ten years at Real Sociedad, five seasons with the professionals, 202 matches played and 53 goals scored, the French player was flying the nest that had nurtured him.

'We would have liked him to stay with us, to continue his adventure with Real, but what could we do? Rumours had been circulating for a long time of a possible transfer to one club or another. His departure didn't surprise us,' confesses Xabi Prieto, number 10 and captain of the Basque club. 'Of the five seasons we spent together, the memory of his meteoric arrival into the first team will stay with me. He was very young and very shy but you could see he had something special: he was quick, obsessed with football and had a goal-scorer's instinct. He aspired to do great things. We immediately realised he had potential, that he would become a great player, that he would go far, but perhaps not so quickly, not to the point that he is already one of the top three players in the world. What Griezmann has accomplished he did on his own. With work and plenty of effort. He was one of the key elements in our return to the Liga and, the following season, he improved, exceeded himself and developed his game. In the end, he went to Atlético, who paid his release clause.'

Atlético were quicker than Monaco and Tottenham in the race to sign Griezmann. It seems the Monegasques were very interested in acquiring the services of the French player but that they did not make an official offer. The English team offered a sum Real Sociedad did not consider to be satisfactory. Finally, after a lengthy negotiation process, the Madrid team managed to come to an agreement for the payment of the player's release clause of €30 million. They met the Basque club's requirements but negotiated so they did not have to pay the €7 million of taxes required by the transaction. 'It has not been confirmed but there had probably been a pact between Real and Atlético since 2011,' claims

Tito Irazusta, a commentator for *Teledonosti*. 'At the time, the president must have spoken to Gil. He told him to "leave the kid alone. Let him stay with us for a while, and when the time comes, you will have priority over his transfer."' Pact or no pact, an agreement between the two parties was reached on 27 July. There was now nothing to stop the player joining the ranks of the Madrid club. 'Atlético made their interest clear a long time ago. They're a great club, with big plans for the future. They're the reigning Liga champions and were finalists in the last Champions League. I didn't hesitate for even a second when I received their offer,' Antoine would confess sometime later. He became the second most expensive player in the history of the *Colchoneros*. Only the Colombian Radamel Falcao, who had come from Porto in 2011 for €42 million, had cost more.

The rumours about Griezmann joining Atlético Madrid had grown more and more insistent, week after week. So much so that, Diego Godín, one of the leaders of the Madrid dressing room, eventually got in touch with the French player through a mutual acquaintance. He told him, word for word: 'I can't guarantee that we'll win titles, but I know you'll like it here with us.'

On 29 July, the day after he said goodbye to Real, Antoine Griezmann signed a six-year contract with Atlético, linking him to the club until 30 June 2020. He said he was very happy and full of hope. He was convinced he had yet to reach his best level, that he needed to learn from his new manager and teammates and that he had joined Atlético in order to continue progressing.

José Luis Pérez Caminero, the director of football at the *Colchoneros*, confirmed that Griezmann 'was the number one priority for the club and his arrival is great news.' From San Francisco, where Atlético had just played the first match of their pre-season tour of America against the San José Earthquakes, Diego Simeone said: 'Griezmann will bring to the team the pace it has been lacking since the departure of Adrián, Costa and David Villa.' It was clear that, as far as the coaching staff were concerned, the French player would be the perfect second striker alongside Mario Mandžukić, newly arrived from Bayern Munich.

On 31 July 2014, shortly after 8pm, under a blazing sun and stifling heat, Antoine climbed the steps to the pitch at the Vicente Calderón Stadium. He was wearing the red and white striped shirt, with the number 7 on the back. Six thousand supporters were sitting in the first ring of the stands. They had come with banners, Tricolore flags and smoke grenades to welcome the young man to his new home in the appropriate manner. Griezmann started with some keepie uppies, like a magician with the ball at his feet, to the delight of the assembled photographers. And, while they immortalised the moment, Antoine took a selfie in front of the stand. On his own at first, then with all the fans in the background. He asked them to stop chanting and squeeze in so he could get them all into the shot. He smiled, made a victory sign, and took the photo. He would later post one of these pictures on his Twitter account. Griezmann played with the public, got them to scream, to listen, and, if the decibels emanating from a particular section of the stand were not up to scratch, he turned to the neighbouring section to get them to roar, offering them a purple ball he had just signed as a reward. Then he spoke his first words: 'Thank you very much for the welcome, I hope to make you happy this year. I hope to give my best and score lots of goals in this shirt.' The club song and chants in honour of Luis Aragonés, a true legend among the *Colchoneros*, brought an end to this first meeting with the supporters. The Griezmann family immortalised the 'ceremony' with their phones in hand. Alain, up in the stands, filmed the whole thing without missing a single second; Isabelle was in tears while Erika soaked up the show. On the way to the dressing room, an emotional Antoine raised his arm and blew a kiss to his nearest and dearest.

Before treading the turf of the Vicente Calderón, the new recruit politely listened to the compliments of his new president Enrique Cerezo: 'It's not easy to find players who offer the same guarantees as Antoine. We are convinced he will settle into the team very quickly. He has the potential to play at the highest level, even if he is only 23 years old. We're counting on him and we're certain we haven't made a mistake.'

It was clear that Griezmann had the qualities to become one of the leading players at the club on the Manzanares, the river that crosses the city of Madrid. It would nevertheless take him several months to show *El Cholo* Simeone what he was capable of.

The Frenchman made his debut for the *Colchoneros* on 10 August at the Volkswagen Arena, against VfL Wolfsburg, in a friendly match. He came on in the 57th minute for Cristian Ansaldi. In the dying moments, he showed a glimpse of what he could do. Tiago slipped the ball into the back of the opposing defence, Antoine picked it up, continued into the penalty area and, with a light touch, passed a perfectly measured ball to Hector, a kid from the Atlético Academy, allowing him to beat Diego Benaglio, Wolfsburg's Swiss keeper.

It was a fine assist for Atlético's new number 7 on the end of a wonderful ball from Tiago. Three years earlier, Antoine had confirmed that he would love to play alongside the Portuguese international. It was now a done deal. Even better, the first thing the Frenchman apparently asked for on arriving in the Spanish capital was a shirt from Tiago Cardoso Mendes. Really? The 36-year-old Portuguese player, a veteran who had played on virtually every pitch in Europe, was delighted. He had begun his career at Sporting Braga before joining Benfica, Chelsea, Olympique Lyonnais and Juventus, and finally laying his hat at Atlético in 2010. 'Yes, it's true. As soon as we met, he told me about it straight away. He said that when he was a teenager, he would go to the Gerland to watch me play with OL. He wanted one of my shirts from my time in Lyon. It was my pleasure, the two seasons I spent in France had left their mark on him.'

On 22 August, Antoine celebrated Atlético's victory in the Spanish Super Cup against Real Madrid at the Vicente Calderón Stadium. In the first leg, at the Santiago Bernabéu Stadium, the two teams were neck and neck, with the game finishing 1–1. During the return leg, only two minutes after kick-off, a Moya clearance made it halfway up the *Merengues*' midfield. Grizi headed it on to release Mandžukić, who found himself face-to-face with Iker Casillas. The giant Croatian did not waste the chance. The match finished with a 1–0 victory for Atlético. For the *Colchoneros*, it was a touch of revenge, satisfaction after the enormous disappointment of defeat in the Champions League final in Lisbon, when a header from Sergio Ramos in the 93rd minute deprived them of a trophy they could already see in pride of place in a showcase at the club's museum.

On Tuesday 16 September in Piraeus against Olympiakos in the first Champions League game of the season, Antoine Griezmann scored his first goal in a red and white striped shirt. It was a shame that it served only to reduce the scoreline and came during the first defeat of the season for Simeone's men (2–3). Atlético's number 7 would wait another month before scoring his second goal with his new team. It came on 22 October, again in the Champions League, during a 5–0 victory against the Swedish team Malmö.

On 1 November 2014, at home against FC Cordoba, the tenth match of the Liga season, the Frenchman scored two goals in the same game for the first time with the *Colchoneros*. Now things were really getting going. In any other team, Griezmann's place in the starting eleven would no longer be up for discussion. But not here, not at Atlético and even less on Diego Simeone's watch. *El Cholo* continued making him climb, step-by-step. He did not yet consider him worthy of the starting eleven. The proof came when he started a game; he would always end up being substituted by Raúl García, Raúl Jimenez or Saul in the second half. And when he did come on, it was often at the end of the match, with only a few minutes left to play. This was the case for his return to the Anoeta (on 9 November, marked by a 2–1 win for Real and the Madrid team's second defeat in the Liga), where it would have been difficult for Antoine to have played the entire game.

In fact, the first few months spent under the command of Professor Óscar Ortega, the physical trainer, had been very challenging. 'To start with', Antoine would say, 'I struggled to breathe and my legs were very heavy. I was surprised by the intensity and concentration required by the Prof and the manager at training. At Real, I was used to the piggy in the middle drill, to working on possession and plenty of laughter. But at the Cerro del Espino [Atlético's training facility], I had to run until I couldn't run any more. It was all new to me, both physically and tactically. I needed time to adapt to the demands of Atlético and to find my place.'

'I don't think Antoine had any trouble, mostly he had to change his position on the pitch. At Real, he played on the wing, while here, Simeone preferred to see him up front, or slightly further back diagonally. He also had to work on the defensive aspect: at Real he made less effort than here, where everyone has to take responsibility,' confessed Tiago. 'The manager always asks us to up the intensity, both at training and on match days. But as far as we were concerned, we saw right at the start that Antoine would become an extremely important player in the team, decisive, capable of winning a match on his own and becoming a leader. But Simeone is a demanding manager and you have to earn his trust.'

Griezmann won the trust of his manager, who can never stand still on the touchline, on Sunday 21 December 2014 at the San Mamés. Against Athletic Bilbao, the number 7, who had abandoned his boy-next-door look in favour of a platinum blond crest on a black background, scored a hat trick to wipe the floor with the Basques. He scored with his head to make it 1–1. The goal to make it 3–1 came after a magnificent piece of control and a left-footed shot that fooled Gorka Iraizoz. He finally made it 4–1 after some genuine opportunism following a strike blocked by Raúl García. This match was a real turning point in his career, a crossroads towards a change of dimension.

From that moment on, the Frenchman was launched at high speed through a season that was entirely exceptional. In January, February and March, he scored eight goals. In April, he scored against Real Sociedad but did not celebrate the goal out of respect for his former club. He retained his honour despite the welcome he received in the form of copious whistling around the Anoeta. The goal against Real, on 7 April 2015, was his sixteenth of the Liga season. He had equalled his total of the previous season. There was more to come: Antoine scored in five of six matches played in April, including two goals on three occasions against Malaga, Deportivo de La Coruña and Elche. These performances earned him the title of player of the month in La Liga, a title he had already won in January, with five goals in three games. The curtain fell on the 84th Spanish championship on 23 May. Atlético finished in third place, sixteen points behind the champions, Barcelona, and fourteen points behind the runners-up, Real Madrid. In the Copa del Rey, the *Blaugranas* knocked out the *Colchoneros* at the quarter-final stage, while Real Madrid took care of eliminating them from the Champions League at the same stage. There was to be no title for Atlético. Griezmann did however clinch one award, preceded by the compliments of Diego Simeone: 'He is the best footballer in the world when it comes to movement and knowing how to find space.' These fine words were followed on 29 May, by the Onze d'Or, a prize awarded by the *Onze Mondial* magazine for the best French player of the year. With 42 per cent of the votes, Antoine beat Paul Pogba (26 per cent) and Alexandre Lacazette (23 per cent). His 22 goals in La Liga, one in the Copa del Rey and two in the Champions League made the difference. They earned him a place as third top scorer in the Liga, behind the behemoths of Ronaldo (48) and Messi (43). Only three players in Atlético's history had ever scored more goals in a single season: the Uruguayan Diego Forlán (32, in 2008–09), the Colombian Radamel Falcao (24 in 2011–12 and 28 in 2012–13) and Diego Costa, the Brazilian-born Spaniard, who had reached 27 goals before leaving for Chelsea. It had been quite a year.

Chapter 22

The Night of Terror

13 November 2015. Horror. The evening had got off to a promising start for Antoine Griezmann. It had been marked in his calendar for some time. The quarter-final defeat in the 2014 World Cup had stuck in his throat for a long time. This return match against Germany – crowned world champions in Brazil after humiliating the host country in the semi-final (7–1), then winning a fourth star against Argentina (1–0) – was timely. There was nothing friendly about this match. It was a chance for revenge, a life-size test for Les Bleus little more than six months ahead of Euro 2016, to be played in France.

Unsurprisingly, Antoine was in the starting eleven that Friday night. Winning his 23rd cap for the senior team, he was on the right wing in the French attack. Strike partners Griezmann and Giroud were joined by the rookie, Anthony Martial, recruited during the summer by Manchester United from Monaco for €80 million (including bonuses), on the left wing. Antoine was no longer a *débutant*. He now had a status to keep up in Deschamps' team.

The start of the season with the France team and at Atlético Madrid had confirmed his growing power. He had already scored seven goals for the *Colchoneros*: two in the Champions League away at Galatasaray on 15 September and five others in the league, including one at the Anoeta in mid-October against his former club Real Sociedad and another match-winner on 8 November against Sporting Gijon. For Les Bleus, he had also responded well, playing his part in a fine series of victories since the start of the 2015–16 season: after a false start against Albania in June (a 1–0 defeat), the French had strung together four wins since the autumn against Portugal (1–0), Serbia (2–1), Armenia (4–0) – with a goal and an assist from Antoine – and Denmark (2–1). They were counting on another two victories in their final matches of 2015 against Germany, on 13 November, and England four days later at Wembley.

The match against Germany took a dramatic turn after the first fifteen minutes of play. The first explosions near the Stade de France came in the seventeenth and twentieth minutes of the game. Two dull noises could be heard while the play was taking place on the left, the other side of the pitch. Antoine cast an anxious look towards the bench with each explosion but as play continued he did nothing else. On the other hand, his head was clearly elsewhere as soon as he was substituted in the 80th minute. From the stands at the Stade de France his friends could clearly see that he was upset, that something was wrong. Had he been told about the explosions that had taken place near the stadium? Or did he just have a bad feeling? What he did not know at this point was that his sister was among the hostages at the Bataclan.

At 9.40pm, while Antoine was toiling against Germany, three heavily armed men burst into the Paris concert venue about fifteen kilometres from the Stade de France, where the American group Eagles of Death Metal were performing their latest album.

As he walked down the tunnel towards the dressing room at the Stade de France, it was almost 11pm. It was at that moment, on TV screens near the dressing room, that Antoine and Les Bleus found out about the night of terror unfolding in Paris: suicide bombers around the stadium, deadly attacks on several café and restaurant terraces in the centre of Paris and the hostage-taking at the Bataclan.

Antoine Griezmann immediately thought of his sister. He remembered she was planning to attend a concert in the capital that night. Les Bleus' number 7 quickly got in touch with his mother. She did not know anything. She had just heard the name of the group performing at the Bataclan on the television: Eagles of Death Metal. Antoine was increasingly anxious and worried. He was clearly afraid for his sister. He tried to find out more about the group online: the Californian band Eagles of Death Metal were from Palm Desert. For fifteen years they had been playing a tough style of music, part hard rock, part garage rock. Exactly the kind of music his sister loved. As far as Antoine was concerned, there was no doubt, Maud was at the Bataclan.

The hours that followed were endless. For security reasons his sister could not be reached; the two teams had been ordered to remain in the dressing rooms at the Stade de France. This made the anxiety even greater. Despite the isolation, Antoine continued to gather as much information as possible, calling his parents and brother, Théo. His teammates and staff did everything they could to reassure him, but, of course, it was not enough.

At 12.10am, the security forces stormed the Bataclan.

At 12.43am, Antoine posted a message on his Twitter account to share his concern: 'Thoughts with the victims of the attacks. God take care of my sister and of the French people. #vive la France'

At 2.55am, Les Bleus were given permission to leave the Stade de France.

At 3.30am, Antoine posted a second message on Twitter, this time to announce his relief: 'Thank God, my sister got out of the Bataclan. All my thoughts are with the victims and their families. #vive la France'

Between the first message posted by Antoine at 12.43am and his departure from Saint-Denis shortly before 3am, his sister, Maud, had managed to escape from the Bataclan. It was shortly after 1am when she made it out of the carnage alive. When the terrorists first came in she was pushed into a corner of the room and found herself face down on the ground, closing her eyes from time to time to avoid having to see the unbearable, completely terrorised by the long silences and the groaning that followed every burst of gunfire. She tried to move as little as possible, to 'play dead' and to stay within reach of her boyfriend, hiding just a few metres away.

When the building was stormed by the security forces, they did not hesitate for a moment. Maud took off her shoes and they ran as quickly as possible, without looking back, to the emergency exit. They spent fifteen minutes running and walking barefoot before they found a taxi. It felt like salvation. Maud and her boyfriend were covered in blood but unharmed.

That night of terror brought the Griezmann clan even closer. A few days after the events, the family took refuge in Antoine's house in Madrid: 'I felt safe at his house, away from the media hype. We're a close-knit family. My mother attaches a huge amount of importance to the love we have for each other. Our closeness has lasted,' Maud Griezmann told *The New York Times*.

A few months after this episode, Maud took advantage of her public relations background to become her brother's press officer at the age of 29. Théo, a former video games geek motivated by Antoine, launched a clothing brand, The GZ Brand, a tribute to his brother, at the age of nineteen:

'We work hard together,' continued Maud. 'We never miss an opportunity to get together at our parents' house in Mâcon. Even Antoine. If he has 24 hours free, he comes home.'

The attacks of 13 November 2015 left 130 dead and 413 injured. They changed the lives of thousands of people and made Antoine keener than ever to spend time with his family.

Chapter 23
Eleven Metres

The penalty, an accursed invention by the Irish textile industrialist, goalkeeper and member of the Irish Football Federation, William McCrum. McCrum came up with it in 1890 while playing for Milford Everton. He wanted to preserve the spirit of the game from the many fouls being committed using hands and feet near the goal. A year later, on 2 June 1891, in a Glasgow hotel, the International Board decided to introduce the penalty into the laws of football.

More than 125 years later, the penalty is still with us, eleven metres from the goal, and it still frightens many players and fans alike. Opinion is divided, however: it delights and fascinates scientists, mathematicians and many others. A penalty can be all that stands between life and death for your team, between winning and losing. The penalty is one-on-one, there are only two possible outcomes, while a football match offers an infinite number of scenarios. Just like life. That is why you need courage to take a penalty.

The Champions League final was held on 28 May 2016 at the San Siro in Milan. *Los Merengues* led 1–0 thanks to a goal from Sergio Ramos, who else? The defender who had crucified the *Colchoneros* two years earlier on a balmy night in Lisbon had done it again. A free kick fired in by Toni Kroos, a deflection from the head of Gareth Bale and Ramos, just two paces from the goal, wrong-footed Jan Oblak as he grazed the ball with a stud. Only the first fifteen minutes of the match had been played. Thirty minutes later the score remained unchanged. Griezmann had tried everything: right foot, left foot, up close and from distance. He got into good positions on a number of occasions but his attempts either ended up in the hands of Keylor Navas or skimmed the uprights.

At the very start of the second half, just after the teams had come back out onto the pitch, Pepe fouled Fernando Torres in the box. The referee, Mark Clattenburg, blew the whistle and pointed to the spot. It fell to Antoine Griezmann to take the kick. The fact that Atlético had made it to the final in Milan was thanks in large part to their number 7. At 25, the Frenchman had become the player that *El Cholo* Simeone wanted: a multi-purpose footballer, capable of defending, pressing, attacking, working for the team, making his opponents' penalty area his own, making the difference in a match and being a precision finisher when it came to finding the back of the net. His season in the Spanish capital had been absolutely fantastic: 22 goals in 38 Liga matches, three goals in the Copa del Rey and seven goals in thirteen Champions League matches. Those he scored against Galatasaray, Barcelona and Bayern Munich were unforgettable. They marked the Madrid team's progress through the competition.

On 15 September 2015, the first matches of the Champions League group stage began. In the changing face of the Ali Sami Yen Stadium, Antoine was a real little devil, in all senses of the term. He delivered a virtuoso performance and left the Turks with nothing to hope for after scoring twice. It was the best possible way to start his adventure.

The second leg of the Champions League quarter-final match between the *Colchoneros* and the *Blaugranas* was played on 13 April 2016 at the Vicente Calderón. Simeone's team had lost 2–1 in the first leg in Barcelona. They had to overturn this deficit at home to avoid being eliminated. The French player scored twice once again. His first came with a header from a Saul cross in the 36th minute. The image is particularly impressive. Antoine jumps up into the air to deflect the ball, climbing so high he was unreachable, while Gérard Pique and Dani Alves could only watch. His second goal came from the penalty spot in the 88th minute of a match that was 'the best of my career from an emotional point of view,' according to Antoine. 'It was extremely tough physically because I had to defend, attack and score.'

On 3 May, Bayern Munich played host to Atlético Madrid at the Allianz Arena for the return leg of the Champions League semi-final. Xabi Alonso gave Pep Guardiola's Germans the advantage with a free kick, putting the two teams level on aggregate. But Griezmann had other ideas. By the centre circle, he picked out Fernando Torres, who immediately headed the ball on. Flirting with the offside rule, the French player penetrated his opponents' half unmarked. The closer he got to the goal, the bigger Manuel Neuer seemed to make himself. 'In my head I was telling myself that what I had to do was open up my foot. So, I positioned myself slightly to the side, moved and eventually shot from right in front of him,' Antoine said after the match. The green giant was beaten. The Bavarians won the game 2–1 but it was Atlético who qualified for the final.

The young man was also more than happy off the pitch. On 8 April 2016, Antoine received the greatest of gifts: Erika gave birth to Mia, his daughter. 'She's so beautiful, I can't find the words,' he told the press. Antoine is the kind of father who sends his little Mia to sleep by murmuring 'Olé, Olé, Cholo Simeone,' in her ear or whispering the chants of the Peñarol supporters taught him by Carlos Bueno. Yes, life had smiled on Antoine Griezmann. That was until the 47th minute of the game against Real Madrid.

Antoine held the ball in his hands. He placed it gently on the penalty spot, eleven metres from the opposition goal. He then turned slowly and stared at the ground as if for inspiration. Keylor Navas had already been cautioned but did not think twice about putting on a show to try to put Antoine off. The Costa Rican goalkeeper had saved on 4 October 2015 at the Vicente Calderón, during the derby between the two teams in the first half of the league season. That night Navas had dived to the left with his right hand stretched up into the air to punch the ball away from danger. On that occasion, *La Pantera* had kept the score at 1–0 in favour of the Real.

With both hands resting on his hips, Antoine waited for the referee's whistle. In front of him, Navas was dancing on the line, jumping, waving his hands, spreading his arms, pushing out his chest to try to occupy as much space as possible.

The Red and Whites' number 7 gathered himself, darted forward and shot with his left foot. 'Boom!' The shot was clean and hard and left no room for questions. The ball crashed against the crossbar, before bouncing off into the distance towards the middle of the *Colchoneros*' half. This time Navas had been unable to anticipate the flight of the ball. He threw himself to the left, as he had done in La Liga. He was completely beaten, but the ball, which had only to slip under the crossbar, smashed against it by just a few centimetres. Antoine was dazed, lost, his gaze empty. He ran a hand through his hair and over his face as if trying to rid himself of the bad luck that seemed to have befallen him.

He was still wondering how he could have failed, how he could have passed up such a great opportunity to equalise. He had chosen power over cunning. Because power was a guarantee of safety, or so he thought. Power would ensure success. Quite the opposite. He had made the wrong decision. 'It was a really tough time for him,' explained Tiago, 'because he had the chance to convert an important penalty. He felt guilty, that was normal. He thought about that miss for a long time afterwards. I never stop thinking about when I controlled the ball badly during the final in Lisbon in 2014, which led to the Real goal. You always think back to those moments, thinking that you've missed a golden chance and you don't know whether you'll ever get another one.'

'For at least a week, I couldn't get that penalty out of my mind. I took and retook it so many times,' Griezmann would admit during an interview with Onda Cero. 'I'm convinced we would have won the Champions League if I'd scored it.'

But it was not the end of the world and Griezmann's match did not come to an end after that wretched 47th minute of play. Although he had not managed to equalise, the Belgian, Yannick Carrasco would take care of it in the 78th minute. The score was still 1–1 at full time. As in Lisbon in 2014, the final was heading to extra time. This time Real Madrid would not be as dominant as they had been two years earlier under Carlo Ancelotti (they won 4–1). In Milan, the match would be decided by those eleven metres, according to 'the procedure for determining the winner after a match has been drawn,' as indicated by the laws of football. It was time for penalties, the lottery, Russian roulette, call it what you will.

Real began.

Lucas Vázquez converted. 1–0

It was already Antoine's turn. You need courage to take a penalty. Particularly when you have missed your first one just a few minutes earlier. Antoine took the ball, placed it on the eleven metre spot and did not break his gaze. The keeper went one way, the ball the other. 1–1. Easy. Gone were the demons that had frightened him so much during his first attempt. But this time the outcome did not depend on him alone. A grimace, a raised thumb and the duel between these two rival clubs continued. The Milanese night seemed endless.

Marcelo made no mistake. 2–1

Nor did Gabi. 2–2

Bale scored. 3–2

So did Saul. 3–3

Sergio Ramos: 4–3

It was the turn of Juanfran, a man who always seems to have a melancholic air about him. He struck the post.

Next up was Cristiano Ronaldo, the *Merengues'* number 7. He had a vision. He knew he would score the winning goal and had asked his manager, Zinédine Zidane, if he could take the fifth and final penalty. It was written in the stars that his strike would wrong-foot Oblak.

'Antoine started crying and we all crumbled,' said Théo, who was sitting in the stands at the San Siro alongside other members of Antoine's family. The emotions were overwhelming when Simeone came over and hugged Antoine in the middle of the pitch. What did the manager say? 'That I had been a key member of the team, that I shouldn't worry about it and not feel guilty about the penalty miss,' Antoine would confess some months later in an interview with *Fifa.com*. 'He told me I had to get back to work with one single aim in mind, of getting back to the final.'

Chapter 24

Euro Diary

Griezmann had just two days to make the transition between the Champions League and Euro 2016, with morale at rock bottom after such a rough night in Milan. After just two days with the family, to rest a little and enjoy spending time with those closest to him, Antoine left for the French training camp in Austria, to prepare for the European Championships, at home in France, in front of his home fans.

31 May

In the early evening, a light rain is falling on the Tyrol when a black saloon pulls up at the Hotel Jagdhof in Neustift in the Stubaital. Antoine, sporting a two-day-old moustache and goatee, quickly gets out of the vehicle. He looks decidedly relaxed in his white t-shirt with black stripes. He has no time to lose. After a hint of a smile and a wave to the waiting cameras and photographers, he goes into the five-star establishment.

The Atlético Madrid striker is the last of the 23 players picked by Deschamps to join up with the squad that arrived in the Innsbruck region that morning. Les Bleus have been preparing for two weeks and played their first friendly the day before against Cameroon (3–2). 'Of course, I watched the match on TV with my friends and family. I'm delighted to be here, it's great to be back with the France team,' Antoine says in his first speech to the journalists.

Didier Deschamps is on the welcoming committee. He

knows his player is not at his best after the final loss to Real Madrid. 'To be honest, I would have struggled to talk to him about how he was feeling after missing a penalty because I've never experienced that, but losing a Champions League final right before an important tournament, that I could talk to him about.' (In 1998, Juventus had been beaten by Real Madrid, but Deschamps had recovered by winning the World Cup). 'I gave him two days to get it out of his system and I was convinced that his smile, good mood and desire would return quickly.'

1 June

Antoine's first training session. Also his first press conference alongside Kingsley Coman and Blaise Matuidi. A proper haircut and an impeccable shave this time before facing the media and putting things right from the start: 'I know there's lots of expectation around me, but I don't want to change my style of play, or how I am. It's the team as a whole that's the star. France won't win thanks to one player.'

2 June

Antoine and Paul Pogba put on a show during an open training session. The two players give the TV cameras a treat with a real circus performance: imaginative ball control, passing the ball backwards and forwards with their heads and shoulders, around the world tricks, blind juggling and volleys with the outside of the foot. They compete with each other in the imagination stakes while demonstrating their clear understanding.

4 June

Against Scotland in Metz, Antoine comes on in the 46th minute of what is France's last pre-tournament friendly. Les Bleus win 3–0 with goals scored in the first half by Olivier Giroud

(two) and Laurent Koscielny. On the right wing throughout the second half, Antoine shows glimpses of promise by
delivering some quality balls to Martial, Pogba and Matuidi.

5 June

The France team moves to Clairefontaine, its base for
the competition. There is barely time for suitcases to be
unpacked before an important guest arrives. Not just any
important guest but the President of the Republic, François
Hollande himself.

Antoine is the third player to greet him after his captain Hugo Lloris and the Arsenal central defender, Laurent
Koscielny. Griezmann is clearly nervous. He rubs his hands
together like a naughty child, not daring to meet the eye
of the head of state too soon. Offering him his right hand,
François Hollande asks simply: 'How are you?' 'Not bad,' the
number 7 replies, timidly. The first conversation between the
two men would go no further.

9 June

Twenty-four hours before the start of the competition against
Romania. Les Bleus pack their bags for Paris's twelfth *arron-
dissement*. In accordance with UEFA regulations, players have
to spend the night before the match within 60 kilometres of
the match venue. As Clairefontaine is 66 kilometres from the
Stade de France, the French team take over the Hôtel Pullman
Paris-Centre-Bercy from the middle of the day. Antoine spends
the final evening before the competition starts with Paul
Pogba, pretending to be NBA stars on their games console.

10 June

The big day. The opening match of Euro 2016 between
Les Bleus and Romania at the Stade de France. That

afternoon during his team talk, Deschamps calls for unity: 'I believe in you and in the whole team.' The manager expects a lot from Antoine, whom he unsurprisingly picks in his starting eleven on the right wing in an attack that also includes Olivier Giroud and Dimitri Payet.

Antoine quickly finds himself with a chance to make it 1–0 in the fourteenth minute. Sagna crosses, finding Griezmann's head. He hits the post. The move summarises his first match in the competition: unremarkable. The Atlético striker is the first player to be taken off by Deschamps, speaking volumes about his performance. He is replaced in the 66th minute by Kingsley Coman with the score at 1–1 (goals from Giroud and an equaliser from Stanciu from the penalty spot). In the 89th minute, Dimitri Payet saves Les Bleus' skin in their first match with an uncompromising strike into the top corner.

France 2 Romania 1.

11 June

A tough night and a score of five out of ten in *L'Équipe* does not stop Antoine displaying his famous good humour. During a bike ride on the Montjoye estate by way of a warm-down, he kids around for the FFF.TV camera: he goes up and down through the gears on his mountain bike, stands up on the pedals and teases his teammates as if nothing has happened.

13 June

'Concerned about Griezmann' reads the title on the front page of *L'Équipe* two days before the match against Albania. It is matched by a full-page photo of Les Bleus' number 7, crouching, staring into the void after missing a chance against Romania, as well as by the caption: 'The expected leader of Les Bleus attack, the Atlético Madrid striker, seemed wiped out against Romania on Friday. Should we be worried?'

There is concern for the player's physical and mental state. Is Antoine burnt out after 54 matches played for Atlético (4,381 minutes spent on the pitch this season, second only to Anthony Martial in time spent playing for his club)? Is he still struggling to recover from the blow of the disappointment of losing the Champions League final? Some months later, again in the columns of the sports daily, the player would look back at this explosive front page: 'It wasn't fair. It was straight after Romania, I'd only played one game.' In the meantime, he would have the opportunity to respond on the pitch.

15 June

During the team talk, Antoine sees the team sheet on the whiteboard in front of him. He struggles to hide his disappointment. Concern and doubt have apparently also affected the manager. His name is at the bottom of the list of substitutes, just below that of his friend Pogba and the OM idol, André-Pierre Gignac. Payet and Giroud, the scorers against Romania, have been rewarded by Deschamps. Anthony Martial and Kingsley Coman are in the starting eleven. The two younger players have been given a golden opportunity but they fail to grasp it: Martial comes off at half time (he will barely play again), while Coman (the better of the two) is replaced by Griezmann after an hour of play.

Time is running out. In the 89th minute, the score is still 0–0. Adil Rami sets off down the wing. The defender uses his stronger right foot to guide the ball. In the penalty area, Antoine jumps up for the header. His touch is spot on as he meets the ball on the diagonal before it bounces just in front of the line and goes over. GOAL! Antoine keeps on running. Bursting with innocent joy. No particular celebration. He just keeps on running before shouting a few words in anger. It is clear to see. Antoine is eventually caught by his teammates, sandwiched between those on the pitch and those on the bench. That goal felt good. Dimitri Payet scores again in the dying moments of the game.

France 2 Albania 0. Les Bleus have qualified for the last sixteen.

Later that night, Adil Rami finds the right words to describe this first French goal: 'My pass was very important because it gave our best player confidence,' he said jokingly. The Valencia defender does not realise quite how right he would turn out to be.

16 June

After a breakfast of champions – cereal, carrot cake and maté tea – Antoine thinks back to his first goal of the tournament: 'I had to be ready in case I was called on. I came back, I scored and it was perfect. And at the Vélodrome! I thought the stadium was going to collapse. It was crazy! It's times like those, given the level of joy and emotion you feel, when there's nothing better than scoring a goal.'

19 June

Switzerland-France, the last match in Group A. First place is up for grabs at the Stade Pierre Mauroy in Lille.

Antoine and Paul Pogba have become inseparable. In the dressing room, still wearing the official France team suit, they try out a few dance steps for the Federation cameraman. It is a way of marking their return to the starting eleven and their understanding is equally perfect on the pitch.

In the seventeenth minute, Griezmann combines with the future Manchester United recruit, who hits the crossbar. In the second half, it is Pogba who cleans up by shouldering his way past three opponents. He passes to Griezmann, who gets support from a teammate before forcing the Swiss keeper to scramble to keep the ball out.

France 0 Switzerland 0.

Les Bleus top Group A; the last sixteen will see them take on the Republic of Ireland, who finish third in Group E behind Italy and Belgium.

25 June

The France team arrive in Lyon in the late afternoon and take up residence in the Hilton in the Cité Internationale. The hotel's rooms boast views of the Parc de la Tête d'Or. The police keep the hundred or so fans who have come to wish Les Bleus luck at a safe distance. For his return to his home region, Antoine has invited his nearest and dearest, getting them seats in the stands at the Parc Olympique Lyonnais where the match will be played the following day.

26 June

It is a particularly restless night for Antoine. Although he tries to stick to his normal routine, not to play in the training match in order to save energy, it takes him longer than usual to fall asleep.

That afternoon at 3pm he will be playing, in his own backyard, in France's first knock-out match, a must-win game.

Antoine is woken by fans shouting under his window. Wearing France and Olympique Lyonnais shirts. 'Antoine! Antoine!' 'Grizou, Grizi, we're here!' He can hear the encouragement loud and clear from his room and, when asked to comment on this potentially dangerous last sixteen match, he says: 'Imagine, if you score in the first ten minutes and you have to keep that going with everyone else behind you.'

It turns out to be a prophetic comment. At half time, the Republic of Ireland cause a sensation leading 1–0 after a penalty converted by Brady in the second minute of the game. It's a nightmare; the French have played a pitiful first half. In the dressing room, senior members of the team read the riot act. Hugo Lloris: 'We're screwing it up. We're afraid. We need to snap out of it.' Didier Deschamps: 'We have to leave everything we've got out there tonight, guys.' Patrice Evra: 'We have to start playing, we're a family, a team. We're going to have to go after the win, we know we have to but we have to do it together. We really have to show them what we're made of.'

Do these words have an effect? Yes, definitely, but they are also accompanied by a radical change in tactics. Ngolo Kanté gives way to Coman to shake things up in attack. Griezmann is repositioned as a playmaker behind Giroud, while Payet and Coman take charge of the wings. The French team and its number 7 seem completely transformed.

A move in the 58th minute gets off to an awkward start. Antoine almost misses a ball that comes in from Matuidi on the left. With the very tip of his foot, he just manages to knock the ball on to Coman, who passes it back to him with a single touch. Antoine then looks for Dimitri Payet, on the diagonal, who switches play to the right following a call from Sagna. The Manchester City defender controls the ball before sending it into the space between the six-yard-box and the penalty spot. Antoine surges forward, gets in front of his defender and brushes the ball towards the far post with his head, past Darren Randolph. The equaliser. Les Bleus have finally got Ireland in their sights. 1–1. This time, when it comes to celebrating his goal, Antoine releases all the pent-up rage and frustration that was visible against Albania. He turns his back on the lost Champions League final and the critics who had followed his performance against Romania. Nothing but happiness. Running like crazy, he even manages to escape Giroud's embrace. A few metres further on, he slides majestically across the turf at the Parc OL. He finishes with the lightning gesture made famous by Usain Bolt. He then puts his thumb in his mouth to dedicate this goal to his daughter, Mia. But his work is not done yet.

Just three minutes later, in the 61st minute, Laurent Koscielny sends a long ball forward towards Olivier Giroud. The Arsenal striker is fond of this type of ball. The pass from his club teammate does not take him by surprise, and as he jumps he sees that Antoine Griezmann is already making a move and understands his intentions. Giroud's headed pass is superb, opening up the path to goal for Antoine as the two Irish players competing with him for the ball in the air leave a huge hole in their defence. All Antoine has to do is get ahead of his marker and unleash a diagonal left-footed shot that he tucks inside the near post.

Goal! France take the lead in this last sixteen game. It looks as if Antoine is about to race the whole length of the pitch. But after a few seconds, he stops suddenly. In front of the south stand he begins a celebration the French fans have never seen before. With his thumbs and little fingers held up to his face he mimes a telephone as his hands and head move in a jerky rhythm. He would later explain that the dance had been inspired by the video for *Hotline Bling* by the American rapper Drake. 'I couldn't do it against Albania because it was too emotional. It was the same for the first goal against Ireland, but after the second, I thought it was time and I went for it.'

France 2 Republic of Ireland 0. Next stop, the quarter-finals.

In the private plane taking the French back to Clairefontaine, the players almost break the speakers with the singing of the disco hit by Gala, *Freed from Desire*. The

Northern Irish supporters had invented their own version during the tournament as a tribute to their striker, Will Grigg. The French now have their own and predictably celebrate their new idol with 'Grizi's on Fire', with Gignac, Jallet, Lloris and the others in unison. Sitting next to Koscielny, Antoine makes the most of the moment.

27 June

After a performance like that Antoine is all anyone can talk about. 'Griezmann was exceptional,' says Noël Le Graët, President of the French Football Federation.

L'Équipe, so critical after the first match against Romania, revises its copy. The newspaper delves back into the archives: 'It was the third fastest double by a French player in a European championship (behind Michel Platini against Yugoslavia in 1984 and Zinédine Zidane against England in 2004). It was also the fastest double in the Euros since 2008.'

Théo Griezmann had gently castigated the sports newspaper the previous day. He celebrated his brother's double with a tweet containing a few musical notes, 'La, la, la, la, la', accompanied by a photo of *L'Équipe*'s front page of 13 June after the Romania game.

28 June

Antoine is the best. Even at Mölkky. A few days before the quarter-final, he pairs up with Morgan Schneiderlin to play the Finnish throwing game outside their residence at Clairefontaine. The game consists of knocking down wooden pins numbered one to twelve. The first to 50 points wins the game. The hero of France-Ireland plays the clown to put Lloris off. It works: the Tottenham keeper misses the target. Schneiderlin is much more skilful. With a hint of irony, the pair celebrate their victory on the Clairefontaine grass.

That night, the French watch Iceland's victory over England in small groups. In Nice, Rooney's penalty is followed by two Viking goals. France will play Iceland in the quarter-finals.

1 July

Ensconced comfortably on the beanbags in Pogba's room, he and Grizi have their noses stuck in their computer. They're playing Football Manager while keeping an eye on the Belgium-Wales quarter-final. Grizi is concentrating; Pogba is unrelenting. The big midfielder launches into an impromptu rap over the instrumental by DJ Grandmaster Flash.

But Antoine is not to be moved. This particular football simulation game is his favourite, one of his main distractions when it comes to passing the time during the long days of waiting. For a few days now, he has taken over from Arsène Wenger in charge of Arsenal. After managing Olympique Marseille and Olympique Lyonnais, he decides to make do with the London club due to the limited financial means of the two French clubs. With Arsenal, he is playing with the big boys and has just won the English league and the Champions League. Not in the real world though, for the moment at least.

2 July

He has two large blisters under each big toe. France's number 7 has not survived the first four games of Euro 2016 unscathed. As a result, he needs an emergency pedicure before the final training session.

After training he has his customary ice bath to aid recovery.

3 July

France–Iceland at Saint-Denis with the final spot among the last four at stake. Deschamps goes back to his 4–2–3–1 and picks Antoine in his favourite position, supporting Giroud. He repays his manager's trust. He delivers a great match from start to finish, his best of the competition so far.

In the twelfth minute, he is the first to congratulate Giroud on his goal to make it 1–0.

In the 29th minute, his corner finds the head of Pogba. 2–0

In the 43rd minute, he provides Dimitri Payet with an assist for 3–0.

In the 45th minute, he scores his fourth goal of the competition with a left-footed jab following a long pass from Pogba, kept going by Giroud.

France 5 Iceland 2.

The semi-finals will see Portugal take on Wales. While France end up with the biggest threat, Germany, the current world champions.

5 July

The benefits of maté tea according to Griezmann: 'I always drink it before training, both in the morning and afternoon, because it wakes me up.'

6 July

Heading south, towards Marseille for the second time in the competition. The night before the clash with Germany, most of Les Bleus are at the Olympique de Marseille training facility. '*Allez OM*,' Antoine says before walking out onto the pitch. That evening, like the rest of the squad, he watches Portugal's victory over Wales in the first semi-final on TV. The goals come from Ronaldo and Nani. Tomorrow it will be his turn.

7 July

Didier Deschamps warns his players during the team talk:

'No one can change what happened two years ago. That's history now, this is the present and future.'

Despite this, Antoine cannot forget the 1–0 defeat in the quarter-final of the World Cup in Brazil in 2014. His tears and the huge disappointment. He well knows that Germany have so often been the tormentors of the French during tournament football. It goes back 58 years. It has to change one day. Would tonight be the night?

Antoine sets the tone at the start of the match. In the seventh minute, he navigates through the German defence, tries a backheel, a one-two with Matuidi and then a low strike with his right foot. Goal? No. Neuer stretches out to push the ball away with the tip of his gloves.

His second strike of the match comes in the 41st minute. This time it ends up in the side netting.

Half time is approaching. Lloris has kept Les Bleus in it with several key saves. One more corner to play and it will be half time.

As is often the case, Antoine takes charge. He sends the ball towards Patrice Evra but the French defender can do nothing, and for good reason. Bastian Schweinsteiger deliberately handles the ball. Penalty! The Stade Vélodrome explodes. It is perfect timing. Just before the break. Antoine refuses to let his concentration waiver. He places the ball on the spot to deliver the punishment.

'This is such an important moment for Antoine Griezmann,' says the leading commentator on French television. The Euros could turn for both Les Bleus and Antoine at that moment. Either way. Looking into the emptiness, Antoine focuses and is off without hesitation as soon as the referee blows his whistle. Six paces and a clean strike. Manuel Neuer goes to his left and Antoine fires the ball the other way, into the bottom of the net. 1–0. He breaks into a repeat performance of the Drake celebration. Then turns to the touchline and shouts '*Vamos!*' into the pitch-side camera, pulling on his blue shirt.

France have one foot in the final. And then soon a second. In the 72nd minute, Antoine scores his second double of the competition. It all starts with some insistent pressing from Pogba, who picks up the ball on the left. The Juventus player, soon to return to Manchester, sees his strike-cum-cross parried by Manuel Neuer. It lands at Antoine's feet, like a gift. All he has to do is take a step forward and strike the ball firmly. 'Grieeeeeezmann!' screams the commentator in ecstasy. 'He takes advantage of the error and scores his second in the 72nd minute! Griezmann is on top of the world. That's it, Les Bleus have just beaten the world champions.'

France 2 Germany 0.

With the game in their pocket, Les Bleus savour the happiness inside the impressive architecture of the Stade Vélodrome. A wall of blue, white and red rises up before them. Thousands of spectators shouting 'Hou!' in unison and clapping their hands above their heads. This sincere communion with the French fans ends with the players jumping up and down in front of their supporters. Of course, Antoine is not the last to throw himself into the fray.

He raises a finger as a sign to his loved ones. He returns to the dressing room and the waiting journalists.

Tell us about these important goals: 'I was keen to take another penalty at an important moment and I'm happy I decided to and that I scored. For the second goal, I was in the right place, waiting for a mistake from the keeper and it fell at my feet. My success is that of all the players, staff and physios.'

Have you already had a chance to make an assessment of your performance? 'Of course I'm delighted, but there's is still one match to go before our dreams can come true. We've got to be ready and I hope for my career that it won't stop there.'

8 July

The number 7's room is a complete mess. Organised chaos with stuff everywhere. Headphones hanging over the edge of a chest of drawers next to bags of loose tea and piles of magazines. Belongings stacked on top of a half-opened suitcase. A computer at the foot of the bed draped with football shorts and a training jersey. It is a good job his mother and girlfriend are not there see it. Only his match shirts seem to have been carefully organised. They are all there. There are also several match pennants, gifts from Deschamps for goals scored. Antoine will leave two days later with an impressive collection.

9 July

The day before the final against Portugal, the France team comes together in the gardens at Clairefontaine for a big barbecue. It has the air of the Bastille Day garden parties held at the presidential Élysée Palace on 14 July. The president of the Federation, Noël Le Graët, says: 'Gentlemen, a big thank you and tomorrow night it's up to you to write history.'

Chapter 25

Missed Out Again

Sunday 10 July 2016

When you have been on such a long journey, made your way through the 24-team draw, avoided the pitfalls of Romania, Albania and Switzerland, dodged an ambush by the Republic of Ireland, calmed the fires of Iceland and, most importantly, tamed the world champions, Germany, it is not for nothing. It is unthinkable that you might fall at the last hurdle. 'The seventh and last step is the most important, the title! That's the only thing you need to have in your head: there's a title at the end of it,' Didier Deschamps hammered home to the players the afternoon of the final match during the team talk in a Paris hotel. 'Guys, you have incredible strength and you have to use that strength to move one final mountain, and you're going to do it together, as 23.'

These words were well chosen, expressed with heart and guts by the French manager. It was a speech to make your hair stand on end. The team talk would not be made public until much later, during the broadcast of the documentary *Au Coeur des Bleus* on the *TMC* TV channel in December 2016.

On Sunday 10 July, the home nation for this European Championship was still focused on a single objective: winning the trophy. There was one man in the frame when it came to them winning the title for the third time, after 1984 and 2000: Antoine Griezmann. The final promised to be his.

As the matches had unfolded he had become the flag-bearer for this France team to which he was now a credit. 'It didn't get off to a great start,' said Vincent Duluc, a journalist with *L'Équipe*. 'He came in on his knees, affected psychologically by the defeat in the Champions League final and we were very worried about his condition after the match against Romania. He complained about us but he may well also have complained about Didier Deschamps, who seemed to share our concern as he left him on the bench for the following match against Albania. Eventually, Dimitri Payet's incredible start to the competition benefited him, giving him the chance to recover away from the spotlight, giving him the chance to get ready in a way he would probably not otherwise have been able to. Then Griezmann scored that goal against Albania. It rid him of his doubts and from the second half against Ireland onwards, he proved himself to Deschamps and was put back in behind Giroud, where he excelled. He was the saviour against Ireland but against Iceland it was clear that he was back to his best. Against Germany he went even further, as only great players can do at this kind of event. So, yes, before the final he was definitely France's number one asset.'

The final would also be all about him because France's opponents were Portugal.

It was manna from heaven for the media who took the opportunity to delve into the maternal roots of the France number 7. The articles touched a nerve: 'A heart-breaking final' that would apparently divide the whole family. The archives were plundered, as with this 2014 interview in which Antoine had said in advance of a friendly against Portugal: 'It's going to be special. I won't be able to help thinking about my grandfather when I step out onto the pitch.'

The TV cameras descended upon Mâcon to gather

testimonies from friends and family as well as the wider Portuguese community. They interviewed the directors of Sporting Club de Mâcon (formerly Portugais de Mâcon), where Antoine's father, grandfather, two uncles and now his younger brother Théo played, They also heard from his great aunt, Isabel Silva, who had stayed in the old country: 'A member of our family is playing for France but Portugal is our team. But I love Antoine. If it's between him and my country, I choose him. I'll be supporting Les Bleus. Antoine has a lot of fans here because we're one big family.'

These snapshots both amused and annoyed the player's family: 'From the moment we knew who would be playing in the final the whole community was interested in him,' said his uncle, José Lopes. 'But he's never really been immersed in Portuguese culture. For example, he never went to the Sporting de Mâcon club. His father was a coach there one year, but Antoine was little. He knows and likes Portuguese food because my mother [his grandmother] lived with him for several years, but he only went to Portugal once when he was eight or nine, to the little village of Raimonda near Paços de Ferreira, that was it.'

'On the other hand', José Lopes concludes, 'there was no question in the family. We were 100 per cent behind France for the final. One of us was playing in the France team. I had to deal with the Portuguese media, who definitely wanted me to say I was supporting Portugal, but of course I wanted my nephew to be a European champion.'

Things were heating up around the Stade de France. Fans of the two teams were flocking towards the Saint-Denis stadium in their droves. The TV channels were reporting around the clock. Passersby had fun making gestures for the camera behind presenters live on camera. '*Allez les Bleus,* 3–0!' said one man in his forties. He was with two boys aged ten and thirteen who, like most of the kids, were proudly sporting Antoine Griezmann's blue shirt. 'Two goals from Grizi like against Ireland and Germany,' said a teenager when interviewed by a journalist.

This celebratory summer atmosphere contrasted with the perceptible calm and concentration in the French dressing room. A few moments before launching their final challenge for the Euro 2016 trophy, Les Bleus lifted their spirits one last time. The rallying speeches delivered by 'Uncle' Pat Evra and the captain, Hugo Lloris, were matched this time by that of Paul Pogba: 'You don't play a final, you win it. Tonight, you're all my brothers and I'm going to fight for each and every one of you.'

The two teams were waiting in the dressing room tunnel. The players instinctively lined up as they came out onto the pitch. This is the moment when they find themselves face to face, in their bubble, away from all the hubbub and noise. The moment you have to make the most of and remember the long journey it has taken to get there. The moment you first meet your opponent's gaze, share a hug with your friends and former teammates, reunite with old acquaintances. Ronaldo was there, at the head of the line. The last time Antoine saw him was in Milan during the disappointment of the Champions League final. The Real Madrid star was wearing the red strip and green socks. With his hair impeccably cut as always, his chiselled face and a look of determination to finally win a major title with his country at the age of 31. Since the start of the competition, he had not been as flamboyant as Antoine, but he had nevertheless saved his country from disaster during the group stage by helping them scrape through into the last sixteen thanks to two goals against Hungary (3–3). Also in Lyon, at Parc OL, he had helped his team during the semi-final against Wales by scoring a headed goal to make it 1–0 and lift team spirits. More than anything, he had played the role of captain, of a leader of men to carry his team into the final as best he could. He was ready for another confrontation with Antoine, the clash of the number 7s: 'The *galáctico* on one side and the rising star on the other,' as the journalists put it.

Griezmann vs Ronaldo. In the pre-match comparison, the statistics seemed to favour the young French player: six matches each but six goals for Antoine and only three for CR7. The Portuguese player had provided three assists, compared with two for Antoine.

Experience was on Ronaldo's side. He had played in the final stages of every European Championship since 2004 and was the only person to have scored at least one goal in each of the last four tournaments.

Thanks to his headed goal against Wales, he had even joined the Frenchman Michel Platini, the hero of 1984, at the top of the ranking of goalscorers in the competition. With nine goals, Ronaldo and Platini moved ahead of Alan Shearer. In fourth place on this list, Antoine already had six goals to his name in just his first European Championship.

The seventh did not seem far off after just ten minutes of play in this game against Portugal. On the end of a pass from Dimitri Payet, Griezmann found himself surprisingly unmarked. He took aim with his head. Rui Patricio sent the ball wide for a corner. The Stade de France was already jumping and chanting the name of its new idol 'Grizou! Grizou!'

Ronaldo grimaced. He was following the action from a distance. He had been dragging his left leg since a clash with Payet in the eighth minute. After just a quarter of an hour of play, he lay down in tears on the Saint-Denis pitch. He was replaced by Quaresma in the 25th minute.

The Griezmann-Ronaldo duel would end there for the time being.

'Despite Ronaldo's exit, it soon became clear that it was going to be very tough for France,' said the TF1 commentator Grégoire Margotton. 'A Euro is so much tougher than a World Cup, especially when it comes to nerves, because there are no easy matches when you can rotate your team.'

'It's true, it didn't look as if Les Bleus and Griezmann would be able to rise to the occasion,' said his colleague Vincent Duluc, upping the stakes. 'It was quickly obvious that one day less recovery time compared to the Portuguese would play an important role in the final.' They were not wrong. At half-time, in Les Bleus dressing room, Patrice Evra shared this feeling that France were not having a good day. 'We're flat, guys. We're flat,' the former Manchester United and Juventus player told his teammates. He took Griezmann to one side and implored him, slapping him with his hand: '*Allez Grizou!*'

During the second half, Les Bleus tried to force the hand of fate with André-Pierre Gignac's golden opportunity at the end of added time. The striker got past Pepe and wrong-footed Rui Patricio, but the ball hit the post.

Before embarking on the extra time that would prove fatal for Les Bleus, Antoine had his chances: in the 52nd minute, he took a corner, but Rui Patricio intervened under threat from Pogba; in the 54th minute, the Franco-Portuguese defender Raphaël Guerreiro took the ball off him right under his nose; in the 59th minute, on the end of a pass from Coman, he failed to strike the ball hard enough to get past the last Portuguese line of defence.

Like Gignac, Antoine also had an opportunity to finish it: in the 66th minute, Coman had just come on for Dimitri Payet. The Bayern Munich winger crossed the ball from the left, this time Antoine got the better of Guerreiro with a header, just six metres out, but it went over the bar. It would have been decisive. 'We've focused a lot on Gignac's chance in injury time, but for me the chance of the final was Griezmann's header in the 66th minute,' said Grégoire Margotton, who, like everyone else in France, was ready to jump up when Antoine struck the ball. 'If Antoine had succeeded, the match would have been over. It was a fantastic opportunity because he is so good in the air. The real Antoine would have made that header count.'

'The final passed him by,' concludes Vincent Duluc. 'He was not the only one, but he did not play to his level. It is in these kind of matches that you can see that football is not rational. Antoine was coming off the back of a huge performance against Germany and who was the big winner in the final? Cristiano Ronaldo. He came off the pitch after twenty minutes and spent almost the entire game on the touchline. It wasn't fair but perhaps it was something Antoine had to go through.'

We all know the end of the story. It was magnificent for Portugal, who lifted their first international trophy. It was tragic for Les Bleus, deprived of the title in front of their home fans. In the 109th minute, Eder scored the winning goal with a low diagonal right-footed shot from 25 metres out. It was the kind of goal that would see a modest striker playing in France with Lille become legendary. It was a terrible way for it to end.

After the game, Antoine was like all the French players: stunned, stupefied, dumbfounded. He searched for some support and comfort from his friends and family in the stands. He understood that once again the trophy had been stolen from under his nose. One month after the Champions League final, he had missed out again.

Portugal 1 France 0.

Chapter 26
The New Idol

The tables were soon tidied away, chairs piled up and the flags left behind by disappointed fans collected. The day after the final, Mâcon, like the rest of France, was waking up with a hangover. Almost 5,000 people had gathered in the Le Spot auditorium at the town's Parc des Expositions to see the local boy lift his first trophy with the France team. Most of them left in silence, lifting their heads only at the sound of horns emanating from cars with the red and green scarves of the new kings of the continent trailing from their windows.

The local kids carry on playing as if nothing happened. On the esplanade alongside the Saône they are replaying the match and reimagining the duel between the number 7s that was cut short. 'Griezmann picks up the ball,' commentates the youngest, a small blond kid wearing a Manchester United cap. 'He dribbles, speeds past Ronaldo and scores from an impossible angle. Grizou wins Euro 2016 for France!' The kid celebrates his dream in front of a goal improvised out of two backpacks before stopping dead to move his hands up and down with his thumbs and little fingers stuck out just like his champion.

France may have lost but Antoine Griezmann nevertheless came out of it a big winner. Despite defeat in the final, he was voted the player of Euro 2016 by a jury of thirteen technical observers, including Sir Alex Ferguson, Savo Milošević, Alain Giresse, Thomas Schaaf and Ioan Lupescu. He also finished as the competition's top scorer with six goals, three more than his teammates Olivier Giroud and Dimitri Payet, who, alongside Ronaldo, was with him in the attacking trio named in the team of the tournament. 'Antoine Griezmann was a threat in every match he played. He works hard for his team. The technical observers were in unanimous agreement that he was the tournament's outstanding player,' announced Lupescu, a Romanian midfielder during the 1990s and now chief technical director at UEFA.

It was clear during the month-long competition, and the 2015–16 season in general, that Antoine had taken on an extra dimension on the pitch. He had become the new idol of the young – and not so young – who enjoyed imitating his game, his celebrations and wearing his blue number 7 shirt. He had become the new symbol of a team that had rediscovered its place in the nation's hearts. Every time he appeared on the official website of the France team he created a buzz during the competition, and the video *A Day with Griezmann at Clairefontaine* broke all audience records on the FFF's YouTube channel (more than 8 million views) and on Facebook, with a surprising number of fans as far away as South America.

'That he should be so loved by the public is down to his normality,' claimed Vincent Duluc. 'He gives the impression that he has stayed the same. You see a lot of young players that start out like that, come into football with a freshness and spontaneity but the environment changes them very quickly. That he should have remained normal is important because normality is usually incompatible with the life of a famous footballer. You can feel that Antoine is not playing a role, he's just like everyone else. If I was the communications consultant for a player, I would calculate everything so that my charge appealed in the way Griezmann does naturally.'

The praise rained down once the competition had come to an end. Antoine was not only a great player and goal-scorer, he also seemed to be a nice guy. 'It is no coincidence that the media and brands are interested in him,' said Grégoire Margotton. 'He is full of positive values, happy on the pitch and not at all pretentious. Even his celebrations, which might sometimes irritate people, have the same naturalness about them.'

French Football Federation president, Noël Le Graët, publicly declared his enthusiasm for Antoine: 'First and foremost, he is a great person. He also communicates well thanks to his handsome face and smile. He's extremely kind. During the Euros, we asked a lot of him in terms of marketing and he always showed up without complaining. He is a great striker who works seriously without ever taking himself too seriously. He still has a mischievous side. Everyone has fallen under his spell.'

Before Euro 2016, he had been voted to appear alongside Lionel Messi on the French cover of the famous *FIFA 16* video game through the EA Sports website. He was also cast in the new marketing campaign for the Beats by Dre headphones brand with Harry Kane, Mario Götze and Cesc Fàbregas. But this was nothing compared to the media frenzy that would follow the European Championships.

First of all came the magazine front pages. Interest in Antoine now went beyond the sports media: *Paris-Match*, *Le Parisien Magazine*, *Sports & Style* and *GQ* took advantage of his new-found popularity to give him pride of place. His exile in Spain had until then kept him at a distance from the wider French public.

Puma, his long-standing sponsor, understood this and played up the personality of its protégé as much as possible. However, in 2014, the sports brand still had him in the background, preferring to use other footballers in its marketing, such as Olivier Giroud, Sergio Agüero and Mario Balotelli. This time, to launch its new deodorant in partnership with L'Oréal, it put the Atlético player on the same footing as its worldwide ambassador, the Jamaican sprinter Usain Bolt. In the advert, the two men run towards each other, face off at a distance and demonstrate the values they share: 'Work, win, celebrate'. The highlight comes at the end: Antoine mimes Bolt's lightning celebration after being thrown fully dressed into a swimming pool then, the moment of recognition for the Mâconnais player, the fastest man in the world mimics his Drake-inspired moves.

It was a *tour de force* by the German sportswear manufacturer, who excelled themselves with a second version a month later. This time Antoine, all grown up, is on his own. He takes on the guise of cupid for Puma and uses his famous celebration to come to the assistance of budding couples. In a variety of funny situations, he appears as a barman, hairdresser, expert knitter and fighter pilot. During shooting it only took him a few takes to get it right. With his nearest and dearest looking on, he shows the same ease and naturalness on camera as he displays on the pitch. But he did not outstay his welcome. He respected his contract to the letter. This new version of the advert was launched in November, and, despite coming out so late in the year, became the most viewed of 2016.

This was only the start of Antoine's success. After this he was voted 'Man of the Year' by the trendy magazine *GQ*. He was also voted footballer of 2016 and the second top sportsperson in France behind the judoka Teddy Riner. In the months that followed, he became an ambassador for the Head & Shoulders shampoo brand and Gillette, as his idol David Beckham had once been. He took advantage of this to (finally) shave off his famous moustache: 'When I saw the adverts on TV I wanted to be a part of it,' he said when his partnership with the brand was made official. 'Lots of football stars have been lucky enough to join the family so when they asked me I said yes straight away!' he continued. 'My look was never all that important to me. My sister would tell me to pay attention to what I was wearing. You have to be presentable. Take care of your hair, your skin, etc.'

His look and physical appearance were now key components of the player's marketing. His social media accounts, gaining hundreds of new fans by the day, revealed his tattoos. A Virgin Mary, a Christ and the initials of his parents on his right arm. The words 'Fame' and 'Hope' as a tribute to his favourite rapper, Chris Brown. He also revealed snapshots of life in his Madrid home: on the sofa watching an NBA game, at a barbecue with friends, or in his car with his girlfriend and dog, Hookie, a cute French bulldog.

Antoine was playing in the big leagues. Sometimes he would lend his face to good causes, such as a campaign to end violence against women. He also lent his voice to Superman in the *Lego Batman* cartoon. The ultimate recognition in France: he almost became one of the performers at the annual Restaurants du Coeur charity concert but had to miss it in the end due to a prior commitment.

The France striker still found some free time to realise a childhood dream at the end of December. He went back to New York, a city he loves. He had spent a memorable week there with his sister, Maud, in 2012. The pair had had fun filming each other incognito around Manhattan. This time he came to the Big Apple with the intention of meeting his idol, the American basketball player, Derrick Rose.

Invited by the French centre Joakim Noah, Antoine was towered over by the Knicks star. The American playmaker seemed not to know who he was: 'Where are you from?' he asked. 'From France, I've come especially to meet you,' replied Antoine, with no sign of any awkwardness. That's Antoine, modest and always enthusiastic. He brought some gifts for the NBA player, an Atlético Madrid shirt printed with Derrick Rose's number 25. In turn, Antoine did not leave empty-handed, thanks to a shirt signed by his idol and an ovation from Madison Square Garden. As is customary, the names of celebrities who have come to watch the match are announced over the loudspeaker. Antoine did not try to hide: wearing a Knicks cap and shirt, he laughed and answered the applause with his traditional celebration. The American public cheered again.

After the match, he shook hands with Noah and Rose. He had no time to lose. He had to get home to Mâcon to spend Christmas with his family. Despite all the honours and his new status, Antoine Griezmann had stayed the same, a kid who had said before the Euros: 'I know who I am, I'm not trying to be anyone else.'

Chapter 27

In Third Place

'Vote Griezmann' said the front page of *L'Équipe* on 20 September 2016. The headline was accompanied by a photo of Antoine wearing the red and white shirt of Atlético Madrid, all smiles, with his hands behind his ears to magnify the sound of the deafening roar of the Vicente Calderón.

The image is accompanied by a short caption: 'After shining for Atlético Madrid, the French striker has taken on a new dimension this year and set his sights on a place among the top three for the Ballon d'Or.' The reasons why France's new idol deserved to receive the most votes were detailed in the accompanying article that made the sports newspaper's position clear. From his meteoric rise over the last two years to two finals, Champions League and Euros, in the same year, not to mention his incredible start to the season for Atlético, when he scored twice in two Liga matches against Celta Vigo (4–0) and Gijon (5–0). His statistics with France were the icing on the cake: 'He finished the Euros as top scorer with six goals ... he is now France's favourite player by a long way (44 per cent of votes in a poll published on 10 July by *RTL* and *Le Parisien*). With thirteen goals in 36 games, he is scoring at a similar rate to Thierry Henry (twelve goals). He is now hot on the heels of a certain Zinédine Zidane, who was the last French player to win the Ballon d'Or in 1998.' Despite this, Vincent Duluc wisely pointed out that 'Zidane was world champion, European champion and was fantastic at the 2006 World Cup, at least until 10.55pm. Michel Platini [winner of the Ballon d'Or in 1983, 1984 and 1985] built his legend on a generation and no one will ever be able to do what he did.'

Once he had been compared to the two greatest legends in French football, the call to 'Vote Griezmann' made Antoine giddy with joy, as he would later admit: 'It was fantastic! I was very proud and happy. I think I even sent a private message on Twitter to say thanks. It was an important gesture and it made me feel great. It made me want to continue working hard and gave me an impetus to give even more.' After the famous 'Concerned about Griezmann' cover that had annoyed him so, this time he was as happy as could be.

But why had *L'Équipe* thrown themselves into a battle that seemed lost before it had begun given the list of favourites in the race for the accolade? To say the least. On one side, Cristiano Ronaldo, who, like Antoine, had played in the Champions League and European Championship finals but, unlike Antoine, had won both. On the other, Lionel Messi, who had just lost in a third successive final with Argentina. After the defeats against Germany in 2014 at the Brazil World Cup and in the 2015 Copa América, the *Albiceleste* player had lost that year in the final of the centennial Copa América played in the United States. Messi, who held the record for Ballon d'Or wins (five titles between 2009 and 2015) had won the Liga and the Copa del Rey with Barcelona, however.

There were, of course, other contenders: players such as Luis Suárez, winner of the Golden Shoe during the 2015–16 season, Neymar, who continued to grow in Messi's shadow, and Gareth Bale, who had led Wales to the semi-finals of Euro 2016.

One thing was sure: there were plenty of candidates and favourites for the 2016 Ballon d'Or. But *L'Équipe* were insistent, buoyed by patriotic sentiment: Griezmann, a French player who was being talked about all over Europe and around the world, could make a nation's dream come true and put an end to years of disappointment by winning a trophy that no French player had won since 1998. The daily newspaper also harboured hopes that changes in the method of picking a winner offered Atlético's number 7 a better chance of victory. In 2016, the Ballon d'Or had been handed back to its founder, *France Football*, after the partnership with FIFA had come to an end. It would now be voted for by journalists, as well as national team captains and managers. At *L'Équipe*, it was said that those in possession of a press card, who had no teammates to support nor any concerns about keeping the peace in the dressing room, would be more objective.

The newspaper was not the only one to support the candidacy of the French player. Diego *El Cholo* Simeone, his manager at Atlético, had been doing so for months. 'As far as I'm concerned, Griezmann has been the best player in Europe. He has scored goals to reach the Euro and Champions League finals and scored in the Spanish league. I hope he will be among the trio of finalists for the Ballon d'Or. He is in great form and has a bright future ahead of him if he continues in the same way,' said the Argentine manager, who, once again, showered his protégé with praise. It was a good way of motivating him and inciting him to give his all for Atlético. Zinédine Zidane, '*Le Divin Chauve*' (the Divine Bald One) and former winner, failed to play the patriotic card, however. He did not share Simeone's opinion and preferred to vote for Ronaldo, his player at Real Madrid. 'It's not because Cristiano is one of my players, it's because he's had an exceptional year. He's done what very few players could do,' he said, before giving his opinion on Antoine.

'He's had some fantastic performances and I don't need to add anything on the subject. He's had a great year and he deserves to be among the best. On the podium? Why not?'

The French did not share Zizou's opinion. In the online polls carried out by newspapers, TV channels and websites, they voted en masse for Grizi. Most of them put him on top of the podium, ahead of Ronaldo and Messi.

The result was declared on 12 December. Cristiano Ronaldo won the Ballon d'Or for the fourth time in his career with 745 points. Lionel Messi came second with 316 points and Antoine finished in third place with 198. He was ahead of Suárez, Neymar, Bale, Mahrez and Jamie Vardy, the two Leicester heroes. It was the second time that year that Antoine had come up against Cristiano and lost: the Portuguese player had also beaten him in the race for the title of European player of the year awarded by the continent's sports media. In Monaco, when he went to pick up his trophy, Ronaldo indulged in a little banter with the French player: 'Sorry Antoine for beating you in the Champions League and Euro finals, and sorry Gareth [Bale] for beating you in the Euro semi-final!'

It would change nothing when it came to the Ballon d'Or vote. Nothing at all. 'I'm finishing behind two "monsters" of the game, two legends,' Griezmann told *France Football* after the ceremony. 'I'm very proud to be in third place.' He had made it to the third step on the podium without winning a single title, neither with the *Colchoneros* nor with Les Bleus, unlike his two rivals. It was his goals, quality football and personality that had seduced the jury. There was only one thing to say: 'I have to keep doing what I'm doing.' In the meantime, he could console himself with an impressive collection of titles won in 2016: top scorer and best player at the Euros, best player in the Liga and the fans' favourite, best

French player abroad (a distinction created by the National Union of Professional Footballers). Finally, on 20 December, he received the trophy for French footballer of the year awarded by *France Football*.

The awards season was coming to an end. The Best FIFA Football Awards was held in Zurich on 9 January 2017. The Best was a new trophy created shortly after the split between FIFA and *France Football* over the Ballon d'Or. Erika, elegant in a long dress, accompanied Antoine for the occasion. Wearing a white shirt, black tie and jacket, the French player posed for photographers, bringing out his Drake celebration and telling journalists: 'It's a pleasure to be here. 2016 has been a fantastic year for me. My daughter was born this year. And as for football, I've had some wonderful experiences with the national team and Atlético.'

With 7.53 per cent of the votes, Griezmann once again found himself in third place on the podium at the end of the gala, behind Messi (26.42 per cent) and Cristiano Ronaldo (34.54 per cent). 'It will be hard to get past these two monsters', Antoine admitted, 'but one day, why not?'

Chapter 28

I Do

Two 'I do's to two love stories in three days. The first, a long time coming, finally happened on 13 June 2017. Antoine Griezmann agreed to renew the contract binding him to Atlético Madrid, extending his relationship with the *Colchoneros* by one more year, until June 2022. The French player's agreement with the Madrid club had recently been reviewed and revised, in terms of both length and payment, most recently in June 2016. But this time the announcement from Atlético, made on Twitter at 1.03pm on a spring Tuesday, put an end to a soap opera that had kept the team's fans holding their breath. There had not been many episodes, there had been no need, as happens in these cases, to wait until late August and the end of the summer transfer window to resolve the affair, but there had been plenty of dramatic, emotional and tense moments. The story came to a head on 22 May. Antoine Griezmann was a guest on *TMC*'s Quotidien programme. Yann Barthès, the presenter, pressed him on his future.

His first question: 'So, where will you be next year?'

Grizi replied: 'That's a very good question. I think it will be decided within the next two weeks.'

'If I said the words Manchester United, like David Beckham, what would your answer be?' Barthès suggested.

'It's possible,' said Griezmann.

The journalist insisted: 'What's the likelihood from one to ten?'

'Six,' came the reply.

'Do you realise what you're saying? Is that the first time you've said that?'

'Yes, it's the first time,' the Atlético striker replied, with a smile.

All the presenter had to do was repeat, or to put it better, confirm what the French idol had just told him: 'A six out of ten chance that you'll sign for Manchester United.'

Was Antoine sincere or was it just a bluff to push up his value with Atlético? 'We are currently negotiating an increase to his contract. We were expecting something like this from Antoine or a member of his entourage. We are convinced that Antoine is going to stay for one more year,' confirmed a member of the Madrid club's management in the columns of *L'Équipe* in response to the bombshell dropped by the French player on live TV.

There had been talk of United's interest in the boy from Mâcon since January. Rumours began to circulate of an agreement between the player and the Red Devils. It was reported that United were prepared to pay the €100 million release clause in his contract and offer him a salary in keeping with what Paul Pogba could expect for the 2017–18 season, somewhere in the region of €17 million a year. It was also rumoured that Pogba, the English club's number 6, had personally committed to convincing his friend to embark on a new adventure in England. José Mourinho would welcome him with open arms and would be delighted to have a goal-scorer of his calibre, a player with so much experience and someone who had never been a troublemaker. There was no doubt that he was a priority for the Special One. So much so that journalists and fans in Manchester had almost taken the arrival of the French player for granted. But it was not just United who were courting Griezmann, there was also Real

Madrid, or at least according to *L'Équipe* on 8 April 2017, the day of the Madrid derby. Their front page announced: 'Griezmann to Real: the secret plan.' Apparently, the darling of French football would be called upon to succeed Cristiano Ronaldo, who would turn 34 during the 2018–19 season. Griezmann would form a deluxe strike force alongside Karim Benzema and Gareth Bale. The French daily sports newspaper was convinced of its sources, even if, just two days earlier on *RMC*, Éric Olhats, Antoine's father figure and adviser, had said a move to Real would be impossible as it would contravene the non-aggression pact between the two clubs. At the end of the match at the Bernabéu in which he scored the goal to secure a draw, when asked if he could rule out the possibility of playing for Real, Antoine answered: 'No, I'm not ruling anything out but I'm happy at Atlético.' More or less the same thing he had told *L'Équipe* back in March when they had offered him the alternative of Real or Barça. 'Why not?' Grizou had retorted. 'It's a dream to play for the biggest clubs like those two, Bayern and the English clubs I've been dreaming of since I was little. But I don't see myself at Barça or Real. Or anywhere else for that matter. I'm happy in Spain, it's sunny. That helps. I need to be happy in my private life. And on the pitch. Because the two are linked.'

So why was there so much insistence and so many transfer rumours about the French player? There were two reasons. The first was that the third best player in the world behind Cristiano Ronaldo and Messi was inevitably on plenty of clubs' shopping lists. The second was the number 7's will to win. He talked about this frankly in an interview with the French magazine, *Le Point*: 'Playing a great match and scoring goals is not enough for me anymore. I want to win titles.'

Unfortunately, titles during the 2016–17 season had vanished into thin air one after the other. Atlético had finished third in the Liga behind Zidane and Ronaldo's Real and Messi's Barça. They had been knocked out of the Copa del Rey in the semi-final by Barcelona and suffered yet another humiliation at the hands of Real in the semi-final of the Champions League. For the fourth consecutive time, after the final in Lisbon in 2014, the quarter-final in 2015 and the final in Milan in 2016, the *Colchoneros* had lost to *Los Merengues*. As in the November derby, Cristiano had once again got the better of Griezmann. In the first leg, the Portuguese player scored a hat-trick that all but guaranteed passage to the final. At the Bernabéu, Atlético won 2–1, including a penalty converted by Griezmann, but Real made it through to contest the Champions League final in Cardiff. Antoine had scored 26 goals in 53 games, a total of 83 in three seasons for Atlético, but at the age of 26 his accolades at club level were few and far between: promotion to the Liga with Real Sociedad and the Spanish Super Cup in 2014 with Atlético. It was not surprising that he should be so hungry for titles and prepared to go to a team such as United or Real, where he believed he could win them. But it was not to be for the 2017–18 season. Things became clear on 4 June when the Court of Arbitration for Sport confirmed the sanction imposed on Atlético by FIFA. Due to irregularities in the recruitment of 65 players at Under-14 level, the Madrid club would not be able to purchase any new footballers until the end of January 2018. It was what Griezmann had been waiting for in order to make his decision. If CAS had allowed the *Colchoneros* to be active during the summer transfer window it may have put the wheels into motion for a move to United, but given the club's inability to find a replacement for him Antoine decided it was not the time.

'The CAS ruling has come through. Atlético cannot recruit. With my sporting adviser, Éric Olhats, we decided to stay,' he said on Sunday 4 June in an interview with *Telefoot*. 'It's a difficult time for the club. It would be a dirty move to leave now. We've spoken with the directors and we will be back next season.' Nine days later, the contract that would take his salary, if the rumours are to be believed, to €10 million a year, was signed with plenty of apologies. Grizi said in an announcement on Atlético's official website: 'The first thing I want to do is say sorry to the fans who may have misunderstood my comments. I perhaps expressed myself badly or allowed people to make headlines where there were none, but since I came back I have given my all for my club, my teammates and coaches and I'm happy to go back for one more season with you all.' Despite the quarrels and threat of separation the love story had reached a happy ending. For at least one more season, Griezmann would yet again be the key player in *El Cholo* Simeone's attack. It would be an important year for the club, which, after 50 years, would be moving from the Vicente Calderón to the new Wanda Metropolitano stadium. However, Antoine's decision to stay at Atlético did have consequences. Éric Olhats split with his protégé. After twelve years, the man who had discovered and advised the Petit Prince moved on. He explained why in an interview with *L'Équipe* on 7 July: 'The recent decisions about Griezmann's image and future are not compatible with how I envisaged our professional relationship. From now on I will focus on my role as a scout for Real Sociedad. I would like to thank Antoine for the faith he has had in me over the years and I wish him all the best in his career.'

Thursday 15 June 2017, Toledo, Palacio de Galiana, 6pm. Antoine Griezmann married Erika Choperena, his girlfriend and the mother of his daughter, Mia. It was a ceremony that took the media by surprise; few people were aware of the couple's intentions. The only clue had come a week earlier in an interview with *Le Point*: 'I know football, it's what I've been doing since I was tiny. A birth or a wedding is something I can't control,' Antoine explained. 'I don't know what will happen when Erika walks in wearing the dress, how I'm going to manage not to burst into tears. It's going to be tough.' The wedding would not be tough but it would be extremely private. Photographers and TV cameras were not allowed into the 11th-century palace on the banks of the Tagus. The only guests were family and close friends, as well as a handful of teammates, such as Juanfran, Koke and Gameiro. Everyone else had to wait to see the newlyweds in a photo posted by the number 7 on his Twitter account. Antoine is wearing a tailor-made navy blue suit and bow-tie while Erika is resplendent in a long wedding dress with a lace train. They are both smiling; as they traditionally say at Spanish weddings: '*fueron felices y comieron perdices*'. And they lived happily ever after.

Chapter 29

Wanda Metropolitano

There are several ways to get your season off on the right foot when you're an experienced striker and a key member of the team: you can score the winning goal to further underline your status or supply a teammate with the right pass to demonstrate your team spirit. But on Saturday 19 August 2017, about 100 kilometres to the north of Barcelona, nothing went as planned as the Liga kicked off …

To everyone's surprise, Atlético Madrid were roughed up by Girona. In the first game of the season, Diego Simeone's eleven went 2–0 down to the newly promoted Catalan team after two goals scored in quick succession by the Uruguayan Christian Stuani. The players from the capital were understandably unhappy and the final result came down to the wire. Cards were raining down in the small municipal Estadio Montilivi: Juan Martínez Munuera cautioned Carrasco, Ñíguez and Hernández one after the other. In the 66th minute, it was Antoine's turn. He was expecting to be awarded a penalty after having been brought down by the local club's goalkeeper right in the middle of the area. The incident would turn the tide of the match. 'Definitely not! Dive!' said the referee, who punished the player from Mâcon immediately. He brought a yellow card out of his pocket, followed straight away by a red. The French international was sent off, for the first time in his professional career. The explanation would come a little later, after the two teams had left the pitch to a final score of 2–2. Despite the Frenchman's excuses, Munuera noted in his match report: 'In the 66th minute, the player Antoine Griezmann was sent off for the following reason: he called me "*Cagón!*" [Chicken!] after being cautioned.'

Antoine would have done better to keep quiet. He received a two-match ban. Fortunately, his return to the team came just in time for the inauguration of Atlético's new stadium on 16 September: it was goodbye to the legendary Vicente Calderón and hello to the gleaming Wanda Metropolitano. On this day of celebration against Malaga, the team in red and white won 1–0 in front of 63,000 fans and the Frenchman became an even bigger part of the club's history by victoriously turning in a cross from Ángel Correa at the near post. 'It's a great honour to be the first to score in our new stadium,' he said as he came off the pitch. 'I hope this goal will be followed by plenty more.'

Unfortunately, the first part of the season passed Antoine by and he did not score another goal in the Liga until mid-November. Things were no better in the Champions League, where, despite a good performance in the fifth Group C game against Roma – a goal and an assist for Gameiro – he could not prevent his team finishing in third place, behind the Italian club and Chelsea. Atlético Madrid, semi-finalists the previous year, were unceremoniously dumped into the Europa League, far from the stars of Europe's top competition.

Moments of satisfaction were few and far between during the first six months of the season. Luckily, there was the France team. Although his play had not been as eye-catching as at Euro 2016, Antoine remained the centrepiece of Didier Deschamps' attacking formation. He was also a guiding light for his teammates when it came to securing their ticket for the next World Cup in Russia: Antoine got things started during Les Bleus' 4–0 thrashing of the Netherlands. Winning his 44th cap, he scored a world-class goal at the Stade de France: after a training ground one-two with Olivier Giroud, he calmly opened up his left foot to slide the ball between the legs of Bryan Janssen. His awareness of goal and finishing accuracy once more made the difference in the decisive qualifying game against Belarus on 10 October 2017 in Saint-Denis. Served this time by Matuidi in the left corner of the penalty area, he won his duel again. France secured the 2–1 win and got themselves invited to the big party scheduled for the following summer in Russia.

With qualification for two World Cups in a row in his pocket, Antoine could now tackle his second challenge of the season: winning a title with Atlético. The choice was limited as his club bid a rapid farewell to almost every competition. In December, they were eliminated from the Champions League and in January, the team from Madrid was bundled out of the Copa del Rey in the quarter-final by Sevilla. There was no point even mentioning the league, in which Barça already seemed untouchable and pushed on inexorably towards a 25th domestic title. There was still the Europa League, a competition Atlético Madrid had won twice in 2010 and 2012, and which seemed clearly within reach.

There was good news for the Colchoneros: Antoine seemed to have recovered his form just as it came to seeking the rewards. In February, he finally lived up to his status in the Spanish league by scoring seven goals in two games: a hat-trick against Sevilla on 25 February, followed by four goals three days later against Leganés. It was a performance worthy of the Liga's greatest and it set the tone for what was to come in the Europa League. The Frenchman lit up the competition from the early rounds: a goal and an assist in the round of 32 against the Danish team FC Copenhagen; another goal and two decisive passes in the round of sixteen against Lokomotiv Moscow and finally, yet another goal at the Wanda Metropolitano in the quarter-final against Sporting Lisbon on 5 April 2018.

Against the Portuguese, Antoine took advantage of an error from the French former Barcelona defender Jérémy Mathieu to make it 2–0. One small footnote: Atlético's number 7 did not greet his goal with his traditional tribute to the Canadian rapper, Drake. This time, he started dancing in a fashion that could well have confused those unfamiliar with video games: with the thumb and forefinger of his right hand, he held up an L to his forehead while jumping from one foot to the other. This choreography was inspired by the hit adventure game Fortnite, which had gained millions of fans since its release six months earlier. Millennials were going crazy for it and the dance known as 'Take The L' was all the rage on football pitches. It was to become the signature move of this new Grizou, who had abandoned his long blonde tresses for an ultra-short haircut.

The job still needed to be finished in the Europa League. Firstly, Atlético had to get past Arsenal in the semi-final. This was to be a special match for Antoine because it would see him line up against his great friend Alexandre Lacazette. The two French players lived up to their reputation on the pitch. The duel was wonderful to see during the first leg on 26 April at the Emirates Stadium. The former Olympique Lyonnais striker narrowly missed the crossbar with a volley not long after kick-off. Antoine responded in the 37th minute with a shot from the edge of the area that was punched away by Ospina; in the 61st minute, Lacazette jumped at the far post to head a cross from Wilshere. The bounce got the better of Oblak. 1–0. Down to ten men, Atlético were not at their best. But in the 81st minute, Grizou stood up to be counted: on the end of a long, deep ball he forced Koscielny into an error. Ospina turned his first strike away but the ball rebounded to Antoine's feet and all he had to do was fire the ball into the back of the net under the helpless gaze of Mustafi. It was a miracle goal that allowed Atlético to content themselves with a narrow 1–0 win in the return leg – an assist from Grizou for Diego Costa – to reach their third European final in five years after two failures in the Champions League in 2014 and 2016.

The final against Marseille was played on 21 May in France, not far from Mâcon, at Olympique Lyonnais. It was a pitch with very happy memories for Antoine. It was here that his career had taken on a new dimension during Euro 2016, when he scored two goals in the win over the Republic of Ireland. It was still lucky for him, it seemed …

In the 21st minute, following an ill-judged clearance from Mandanda and a poor piece of touch from Anguissa, Grizou punished the Olympique de Marseille keeper with an unstoppable left-footed shot. 1–0.

In the 49th minute, thanks to an assist from Koke, Antoine once again made it into the penalty area to score his second with a magnificent flick of his left foot. 2–0.

In the 89th minute, Gabi inflicted the final blow, with a calm, diagonal shot just inside the box. 3–0.

Atlético had delivered a demonstration and Antoine had broken his jinx after losing two finals in 2016. He savoured this first European title on the pitch, with all his family gathered around the cup. The Frenchman was unquestionably the Man of the Match, with two goals that brought his total to 29 for the season in a Colchoneros shirt. It had not been a perfect year, but for Antoine the final made it worthwhile:

'It's a reward for all my efforts since I left home at fourteen. A lot of work, suffering, joy and sadness. I'm really happy tonight. It was great, with all these fans. We're going to enjoy it, celebrate it properly and forget the season. And think about the World Cup.'

But there was still one important detail to be settled before thoughts turned to Les Bleus. And it could hardly have been more important. Where would Antoine be playing next season? 'I don't think this is the right time to talk about my future,' said the hero of the final dismissively after the game. But Atlético's supporters would have liked an answer. They were starting to get tired of the same old story. After Manchester United the previous season, it was now Barcelona who seemed intent on wooing their number 7. Barça were said to be ready to put €100 million on the table to meet Antoine's release clause. Leo Messi was already waiting for the French player: 'It's easy to get along with great players and Griezmann is one of the best. This is an exceptional time in his career. It would be up to the manager to decide how we played together, but he's a great player and we would get along perfectly on the pitch.'

Despite this appeal from the Argentine star, the suspense dragged on for more than a month. Atlético made plenty of effort to convince their player to stay. President Enrique Cerezo had a contract extension until 2023 up his sleeve and above all an increase in Antoine's salary that would bring it up to €23 million per season. There was plenty to think about …

The news finally came on 14 June 2018, two days before France's first World Cup game. And, because Antoine always likes to be different, he decided to announce his decision in a documentary broadcast on the Spanish channel Cero de Movistar+. It was somewhat surreal: in the half-light, he faces the camera, like a boxer, with a black hood over his head. He then gradually turns his back to the lens as the Wanda Metropolitano stadium comes into view behind him. He would be staying at Atlético. He was clearly happy and relieved. To share his happiness, the video was accompanied on social media by a message: 'My fans, my team, MY HOME! @atleti'.

Chapter 30

The Star

The star. At last. The one they had been longing for for twenty years. The gold star that sweeps away disappointments, criticism and memories of finals lost. The star that makes you cry so hard you have to bury your nose, or even your whole face, in your blue shirt. But this time, they were tears of joy. Not of sadness or anger, as they had been in Paris in 2016 – after the goal from the Portuguese player Eder in the 106th minute – or in Milan, in the Champions League final, after that penalty that struck the crossbar. This time there was the star: Grizi, drenched by the Russian downpour, shows it off, smiling, pointing at his brand new jacket, fresh out of the packet. Next to him is Kylian Mbappé, the revelation, pointing at what he too had always dreamed of. Behind them stands Paul Pogba, the joker, surprised, with his mouth wide-open, pointing his finger at the star over the number 7's shoulder, as if to tell the world they had done it: they were world champions, just like Zidane and Co. in 1998. They had given France its second star.

Two days before the final against Croatia, Antoine Griezmann had said: 'I want the star and if I get it, I don't care how!' He did get the star, in his own way, in Didier Deschamps' way. He may have won the Golden Boot at Euro 2016, scoring six goals, but he had lost the final. As he explained, with a smile: 'I was top scorer but we still lost. So I said to myself: "I'll score fewer goals to see if we win this time."' And win they did. Antoine was the best player in the final, something that was recognised by FIFA on Sunday 15 July at the Luzhniki Stadium in Moscow: Man of the Match. As well as the star, it brought great satisfaction to the skinny little boy no one in France had wanted, to the 27 year old whose titles had been few and far between prior to 2018. There was no doubt: the Russia World Cup had been his revenge, his consecration. A World Cup in which things had improved from match to match.

Grizi had not started well, nor had the France team as a whole; they almost got the tournament off on the wrong foot against Australia in Kazan on 16 June. Les Bleus eventually beat the Socceroos 2–1 but had VAR and goal-line technology to thank. Andrés Cunha, the Uruguayan referee, had failed to spot that the sliding Josh Risdon had taken out Griezmann's ankle rather than the ball. It was pointed out to him and, after seeing footage on the pitch-side TV, he blew his whistle for the first VAR penalty in World Cup history. Antoine made no mistake from the spot in the 58th minute.

The team in yellow went on to equalise – with another penalty thanks to a wayward hand from Samuel Umtiti – before goal-line technology came to the rescue of the French. As Pogba and Behich clashed, the ball flew up, hit the crossbar, went over Ryan, the goalkeeper's head and landed just a few inches over the white line. Cunha looked at his watch as it alerted him to the goal and blew his whistle. In the 80th minute, France breathed a sigh of relief and Antoine celebrated. From the bench. Deschamps had replaced him with Olivier Giroud fourteen minutes earlier. It was a change he was not altogether delighted about.

At the end of the game, France's number 7 was named Man of the Match, but he himself confessed that the award would have been better given to N'Golo Kanté or Lucas

Hernández. He was not happy with how he had played and he admitted it to the TF1 and BeIN Sport microphones: 'There's no doubt I want to play better.' And if he was unhappy, it was not hard to imagine what the French media thought. His performance was judged at between three and four and a half out of ten. 'Disappointing' was the most widely used word. Given his age and international experience, the most was expected of him in the three-pronged attack (Griezmann, Mbappé and Dembélé) deployed by Deschamps in the first game. He had been neither conductor, nor finisher nor out-and-out striker. He had wandered from left to right, taken free kicks, tried some headers or shots from outside the box, but in the end, he had only the penalty conversion to his credit. He had failed to shine and seemed to have little understanding with the other two forwards. Some justified it by claiming he was tired after a long season; others lamented the absence of Giroud, of a battering ram like Diego Costa for Atlético Madrid, someone to keep central defenders occupied and leave him plenty of easy chances to sweep up. The fact was that, from France to Germany and from Spain to Italy, many doubted whether Les Bleus had any chance of winning the title playing like that.

Doubts that were not swept away by the second game against Peru. 'What's going on with Griezmann?' was the *Sport* headline, tinged with malice, given that the boy from Mâcon had eventually decided to stay at Atlético. But the Catalan sports daily was not the only media outlet to get stuck in; the French press did not hold back and Grizi's performance received more or less the same rating as the first match, as everyone lamented that the boy from Mâcon was not the leader they had all been dreaming of. Deschamps had rebuilt his team around the 'Petit Diable', whom he considered his leader up front, behind Giroud, in for Dembélé, who had been fragile against Australia. Giroud the Giant did his job against the South Americans: in the eleventh minute, he sent a promising ball towards Grizi but the running number 7 fired it well wide of the post. History repeated itself in the sixteenth minute, as the Chelsea striker's header laid the ball off perfectly for Antoine, but the Madrid player's shot struck the knees of the Peruvian number 1, Pedro Gallese. There was little else to report. In the second half, he seemed so absent that his manager recalled him to the bench in the 79th minute and sent on Fekir. Thanks to a goal from Mbappé into an open net, France qualified for the last sixteen with a game in hand, while Peru's World Cup was already over. But it was far from impressive.

The final Group C game against Denmark in Moscow on 26 June ended with a soporific 0–0 draw. Zero entertainment, zero goal-scoring opportunities. Neither of the two contenders were keen to overexert themselves and they both got what they wanted: France secured first place in the group, with Denmark second. Griezmann was on the pitch until the 70th minute, when he was substituted, once again by Fekir. What about his performance? Flat, transparent and inconsistent. To sum up, so far he had not been the motivator, leading man or superstar. But his teammates believed in him. Captain Hugo Lloris said: 'I think the knockout games are better for Griezmann. He will raise his level because he feels he's one of the best at the World Cup.' Didier Deschamps admitted Grizi had got off to a difficult start, but was convinced he would be at his top level against Argentina.

On Saturday 30 June, the nineteen-year-old Kylian Mbappé, the PSG phenomenon, sent Leo Messi and his dreams of winning a World Cup home. The Petit Prince flew across the pitch of the Kazan Arena, leaving the Gauchos' defenders in his wake and scoring two goals. He received admiration from all over the world, as well as flattering comparisons with Pelé and Ronaldo, the Brazilian. What about Antoine Griezmann? This time he had lived up to expectations. He was not the bolt out of the blue the number 10 from Bondy had been, but he was the man who had got the party started and played the role of metronome. In the ninth minute, his free kick almost broke the crossbar. In the thirteenth minute, he made no mistake in front of Franco Armani: the keeper went left, the ball went right. The conversion of the penalty awarded for Rojo's foul on the speeding Mbappé was perfect. The number 7 rediscovered his touch against Messi and Co., calling for ball after ball all over the pitch: in the box, on the wing, tracking back to lend a hand in defence and in front of goal. When he gave up his place to Fekir in the 82nd minute, his exit was applauded. Finally, even the reporters recognised the work he had put in. He was awarded a high mark that was far from excessive in what had been a fantastic match, the best France would play in Russia. It ended 4–3 as Messi bowed his head. The sceptre of world football was no longer his. It was the turn of the Griezmann–Mbappé generation to take things forward.

The path to the final was blocked by the Uruguay of Óscar Tabárez and Antoine's mentor Diego Godín. 'Diego is a great friend. I'm with him every day, in the dressing room and on the pitch,' said Antoine. 'He's godfather to my daughter. If I stayed at Atlético, it's because of him.' Diego and Uruguay: two of Antoine's real passions. Since his boyhood days at Real Sociedad, when he would stay after training with Carlos Bueno, he had always had a Uruguayan by his side, helping him and teaching him the ups and downs of football and life. He had also learned to appreciate *mate* and to love and respect Charrúa culture, something he demonstrated on 6 July in Novgorod.

In the 61st minute, France were 1–0 up against La Celeste thanks to a header from Raphaël Varane, when Grizi found himself with the ball on the edge of the area. His central shot was fumbled by Muslera but the ball flew up oddly before finishing in the back of the net. It was a gift of the kind given by Loris Karius to Real Madrid or David de Gea to Portugal. It was 2–0 and the goal was the final nail in the coffin for the comeback hopes of a tired Uruguay, without the injured Cavani. The French fans in the stands made merry but Grizi chose not to celebrate the goal out of respect for his Uruguayan friends.

The semi-final would be tough. France faced Belgium, who had matured thanks to the tactical magic of the Spaniard Roberto Martínez and the attacking advice of the exiled Thierry Henry. They were a golden generation that had sent O Rei Neymar's Brazil packing against the odds. Things did indeed seem very tough to begin with: no one could keep Eden Hazard quiet, Mbappé was well shackled and it was not Griezmann's day. But then, as usual, a French defender stepped up. Not the young Pavard, who had pulled off an incredible goal against Argentina, nor Real Madrid's Varane; this time it was the turn of Umtiti to solve the equation. A header from a corner that was covered poorly by Marouane Fellaini and the goal came six minutes into the second half. Then it was everyone back to defend Les Bleus' 1–0 lead tooth and nail. Including Griezmann.

France looked more like Italy, playing *catenaccio* and smothering counter-attacks, taking El Cholo's Atlético Madrid style into the final in Moscow. Didier Deschamps had learned well at Juventus. Few frills, simplicity and to hell with tiki-taka or possession: France parked the bus, forming a solid block that defended well, exploiting long balls and counter-attacks. Grizi explained it well in the press conference on the eve of the final: 'In our style of play and with the players we've got, defence is the most important thing. We can make something happen with our strikers, Kylian on the break, Olivier with a cross or me, with a little bit of madness, as happens from time to time.' When they asked him if this France team was playing in the style of Atlético, he answered: 'I'm lucky enough to work with the best defensive manager [Diego Simeone]. I see things on the pitch and I try to talk about them, to teach them, just as they can teach me little things up front, I give them advice and tricks for changing things defensively.' He went on: 'My game changes. I'm more about creating rhythm, keeping the ball and accelerating. If I score, even better! But I'm more a player who thinks about the team than about scoring my own goals.' Was he proud that people were now talking about the Griezmann Generation? 'I'm sure I'll be proud later on, but I always put the group first. You can't do anything without the group. We talk about Zidane's '98 generation. I don't know who it will be in 2018, it doesn't matter. I just want us to play a great match and win the World Cup.'

And that was exactly what happened. Griezmann, like Zidane on 12 July 1998, was the best of Les Bleus. He made the difference when France were put under the cosh by the Croatians, led by Luka Modrić and an Ivan Perišić who was playing like a man possessed. Antoine's left-footed free kick was deflected into the goal by Mandžukić. They had failed until then to create even one scoring opportunity yet, thanks to Grizi, Deschamps' boys found themselves in the lead. He also put them back in front after Perišić had levelled things up. He did not allow himself to be put off from the penalty spot by Subašić's fidgeting. It was his third penalty and fourth goal of the World Cup. Then it was the turn of his comrades from the photo with the star, Pogba and Mbappé, to finish things off. With the final score at 4–2, it was time only for tears and celebrations under the pouring rain of Moscow and the heat of Paris. Grizi had wanted the World Cup and he had succeeded in lifting it. He had wanted the second star on his shirt and he had achieved it. Who knows whether, as it was for Zidane, he will one day be able to add a Ballon d'Or to his trophy cabinet?

Acknowledgements

We would like to thank the following people: Kodjo Afiadegnigban, Luis Arconada, Jagoba Arrasate, Nere Azurmendi, Juan-Antonio Aldeondo, Philippe Alves, Stevie Antunes, Franck Arlabosse, Óscar Badallo, Guillaume Bigot, Stéphane Blondeau, Carlos Bueno, Vincent Cabin, Xavier Chavalerin, Bruno Chetoux, Manu Christophe, Thierry Comas, Marc Cornaton, Iñigo Cortés, Julian De Cata, Pietro De Cata, Théo Defourny, Francis De Taddéo, Anthony Defois, Serge Delmas, Cyrille Dolce, Vincent Duluc, Francis Dupré, Alain Duthéron, Sébastien Faure, Gérard Fernandez, Jean-Michel Foucher, Gérard Francescon, Philippe Gastal, Jon Gaztañaga, Miguel González, Christophe Grosjean, Catherine Guérin, David Guérin, Paul Guérin, Mauri Idiakez, Andoni Iraola, Tito Irazusta, Luki Iriarte, Meho Kodro, Martín Lasarte, Pacheco Leal Antero, José Lopes, Roberto López Ufarte, Daniel Maraval, Grégoire Margotton, Tiago Mendes, Jorge Mendiola, Juanan Mentxaka, Jean-Baptiste Michaud, Pierre Michaud, Philippe Montanier, Patrice Montheil, Sébastien Muet, Philippe Nanterme, Pierre Nogues, Javier Olaizola, Laurent Perraud, Nathalie Perraud, Bernard Pichegru, Xabi Prieto, Enzo Reale, Diego Rivas, Serge Rivera, Stéphane Rivera, Iñigo Rodríguez, Gilles Rouillon, Josean Rueda, Alex Ruiz, Peïo Sarratia, Dennis Schaeffert, Gilles Signoret, Francis Smerecki, Julien Sokol, Jean-Jacques Verseau and Martin Voir.

Thank you to Michael Sells, Duncan Heath, Philip

Cotterell, Laura Bennett, Laure Merle d'Aubigné and Roberto Domínguez.

Thanks to Céline, Elisa, Elvira and Lorenzo for their support and valuable advice.

Thanks to Yvon Marcellin for his work.

Thanks to Javier Villagarcía (Tas Production) for his contacts.

Finally, happy reading to Arthur, Jules, Colin, Tom, Louis, Benjamin and Nolan.

This book is dedicated to Mathieu and Olmo in memory of a great evening at the Vicente Calderón.